IMAGES OF ENGLAND

PENRYN
REVISITED

IMAGES OF ENGLAND

PENRYN
REVISITED

ERNIE WARMINGTON

TEMPUS

Cancer Research UK is very grateful to Ernie Warmington who kindly donates all of his royalty proceeds to our vital research. Our scientists have discovered new ways of beating cancer that have saved hundreds of thousands of lives. There is still much to be done and our groundbreaking work, funded overwhelmingly by support and donations, will ensure that millions more people survive.

Frontispiece: With a white-faced town clock and the trees in full leaf, this postcard is dated 1914. The hut under the tree was used by the cab drivers that parked their cabs outside the Wesleyan chapel to the right. On the left is the Elephant & Castle Hotel. Just down a little further, opposite the horse-drawn wagon, is St Gluvias Street which leads to Commercial Road and St Gluvias Church.

First published 2007

Tempus Publishing
Cirencester Road, Chalford,
Stroud, Gloucestershire, GL6 8PE
www.tempus-publishing.com

Tempus Publishing is an imprint of NPI Media Group

British Library Cataloguing in Publication Data.
A catalogue record for this book is available from the British Library.

ISBN 978 0 7524 4607 3

Typesetting and origination by NPI Media Group
Printed in Great Britain

Contents

Acknowledgements

Penryn, I am proud to say, is where I was born in 1935, at Bennetts Yard shortly after moving to No. 83 The Terrace where I lived with my parents and brother Reggie. No matter how much you think you know about your home town, where you were schooled and brought up, you will never know everything about the place, however there is always someone who you can turn to for more information. It is these people I acknowledge for the help they have given me in the way of naming people and places and remembering where and when events happened and the little tales that go with them. This is my third book about Penryn with at least another to follow at a later date. Once again the royalties (minus a few expenses) go to Cancer Research. For any names I have spelt incorrectly or anyone I have missed out, any places or dates I have got wrong, I apologise. This book has been written with my knowledge about my home town. My thanks go to everyone who helped me to compose the book, especially my wife Rosemary for typing the text and putting up with a disrupted household for some considerable time. Once again the book is dedicated to my parents and brother Reggie.

If you would like a copy of any of the contents of this book, for a small donation to Cancer Research, I will oblige you with a copy. (Contact through Tempus Publishing.)

My thanks to the following: Mary May (Mayor of Penryn), Kevin Paul (Penryn town clerk), S. Richards, Revd G. Warmington (cousin), T. and P. Kerslake (cousins), W. and T. Toy, G. and R. Collings, J. Basher, T. Dungate, Mrs R. Hodges (family), R. Blake, R. Doney, J. Tregonning, R. Webber, A. Gosling, R. Woods, D. Owen, V. Tullin, K. Newell, I. Symons, H. Minter, M. Rich, Dr Dommett, J. Driscoll, C. Lang, F. Squibb, C. Cole, I. Dodd, Mrs Willy, J. Hingston, R. McCall, Mrs Hilda Carter, S. Brimicombe, J. and D. Bassett, B. Richards, I. Butland, T. Roberts, B. Quintrell, M. Edwards, J. Miller, M. Boase, R. Hold, S. Bennett, C. Tremayne; C. Spencer.

Introduction

Penryn is an attractive town of character, charm and much history and lies at the head of the river that flows into the Falmouth Harbour. The town covers 900 acres, has a population of about 6,000 and can trace its history back to the Saxon times; it was of such importance it was recorded in the Domesday survey of 1086. Penryn was founded as a town by an Italian Bishop of Exeter, Simon de Apilia, in 1216 and the first charter for markets was granted in 1236. Sampson Bloyes was the first mayor and the town received its first charter as a borough during the reign of James I in 1621.

The real beginning however resulted from the building of the great Collegiate church of St Thomas at Glasney in 1265 by Walter Bronscombe, the Bishop of Exeter, experiencing a dream during an illness to build this religious college on marshy land at Glasney. It was built in two years using local granite and labour as well as stone from Caen in Normandy. The church was documented in 1334 and built on a six-acre site. It was defended from surprise attacks by French and Spanish pirates with its fortified towers and a chain boom across the head of the creek. This established the town as an ecclesiastical capital of Cornwall. Had the priory not been closed and suppressed during Henry VIII's Reformation, Penryn without doubt would now be Cornwall's cathedral city instead of Truro. Edward VI, in 1547, ordered the complete dismantling of the church, selling the buildings and shipping the lead to the Isles of Scilly. The better and more finely worked stone was used to build prominent buildings and homes locally. There are many carved stones preserved and on display in the town's museum. In the fourteenth century, as a sea port, the town had little trade but later in the Tudor years it became one of the principal ports in Cornwall and with others in the area had recorded more shipping than many other ports in the country.

1488 saw Henry VII send a Cornishman, Sir Richard Nanfair, with others to seek an alliance with Spain and brought back Princess Catharine of Aragon to marry his son, Henry VIII. Running into a great storm and tempest they had to shelter in Falmouth Harbour, and with nowhere to stay they came to Penryn residing at the King's Arms for nine days until the storm subsided. Eighteen years later, whilst sheltering from another storm in 1506 at Penryn, the Venetian Ambassador to Castle, King Phillip and Queen Juana wrote home to say he was, 'staying in a very wild place which no other human beings ever visits, in the midst of a most barbarous race, so different in language and customs than the rest of England …'.

In 1621 when the first charter was granted in the reign of James I, the lawless of Penryn was notorious, the town's many inns, taverns and breweries fuelled the regular fights and riots and even pickpocketing and prostitution was rife. Smuggling and piracy had long been an issue. The charter read:

> To the Maritime and Ancient Populous Borough occupying and exercising a market in and upon the sea by reason of the exportation and importation of goods and merchandise the aforesaid borough through indolence for a long time in the arrival of sailors and other unruly men working together, divers, riots and routs, also very many great offences are there often committed and perpetrated. The town has requested a Mayor and Corporation to administer the laws of the land so that the borough shall remain a borough of peace and quietness to the dread and terror of evil doers.

Later in the seventeenth century, with the development of the tin and copper mining industry in the Camborne-Redruth area, prosperity again came to Penryn with the port handling huge amounts of exports and imports. These included tin, copper, flour, gunpowder, fruit, meat, timber, cattle, Peruvian guano, coal, wool etc., but it was short-lived when Sir Walter Raleigh returned from his voyages of discovery in the West Indies and stayed at Arwenack House, the home of the Killigrews. He saw the need for the supply of food and lodgings for returning seafaring men in the area. Sir Peter Killigrew, a businessman, saw this potential and managed to move the customs due from Penryn to the newly developed hamlet of Penny-Come-Quick. Penryn and Truro petitioned the King, but James I agreed to the new town of Falmouth which was granted its first charter in 1661, making Penryn 400 years older than the new upstart Falmouth. Again it caused a serious decline in trade for Penryn, however the early nineteenth century saw the start once again of prosperity coming to the town in the way of a granite industry. A Scotsman named John Freeman set up a business alongside the Penryn River with huge deposits of the finest granite lying just below the ground's surface in the small villages around Penryn. The stone was quarried and brought to the works at Penryn, first by horse and cart, then by traction engine and eventually using their own petrol-driven lorries. Penryn then became known as the 'Granite Port'. From these works and quays were shipped large quantities of shaped stone for shipyards, London buildings, and monuments in this country as well as abroad. It became a huge industry, employing hundreds of men in the quarries at Constantine, Mabe, Longdowns and other towns and villages as well as the yard on the Falmouth Road.

With the amount of foreign shipping coming in to the port of Penryn in the 1800s also came trouble with rioting, fighting and prostitution around the many of the inns, taverns and ale houses which stood only a few yards away from Exchequer Quay. There was the Anchor at Quay Lane at the top of Bole Hill Street (Quay Hill and Bo-Hill as we know them) and near The Square was the Swan Inn. The Crown was in St Thomas Street and the King's Arms was in Broad Street, where, further up was the Golden Lion. Reports printed in the local papers around 1840 state that in several Cornish towns a gentlemen would be accosted by at least forty prostitutes within a few hundred yards, so it only concludes Penryn must have been the same if not worse.

In August 1869, *The West Briton* reported:

No town in the Western Counties has been flourishing more during the past year as Penryn. Its steam engines are working flat out employing large numbers of men earning 5-6s per day. Two thousand, five hundred head of cattle have been imported plying constantly between Penryn, Spain and France. An iron foundry established a few years ago by Mr Sara has been fully employed, Mr Mead's paper mills were also doing well. The potato trade has not done so well as former years owing to the excellent English crop. The fruit trade from the orchards and gardens were finding a ready trade from the great number of vessels constantly arriving and departing the port. Tanyards, coal stores, lime kilns and flour mills also placed the town commercially in a very healthy state.

A health report of Penryn of around 1870 stated that the gutters in many instances were placed so that the fluids soaked into the foundations of the houses whilst there was a groove cut into the centre of the pavements for walkers. House slops and liquid filth filled the air with a stench. The roads were in great neglect with stagnant pools, decomposing vegetables and other filth. It was customary and even more disgusting to people to empty the contents of privies, middens and cesspools into the streets leaving the excreta there until it was carted away. With the exception of a few large houses which were provided with WCs, all other dwellings had privies and uncovered middens. From one end of the borough to the other the inspector found a condition of utter sanitary neglect. Behind the houses and lining the streets were tons of filth, refuse and poverty. Many of the cottages were unfit for human habitation.

The 1900s came and with it the two world wars where many hundreds of brave men left Penryn to fight for their country. Many didn't return, those that did went back to their old jobs with Freeman's and other firms in the area.

The era of concrete saw the decline in the granite trade and Freeman's closed in 1965. The quarries still produce stone for facing buildings, road building and for reconstituted stone produce. (see more about Freeman's with photographs further on in this book).

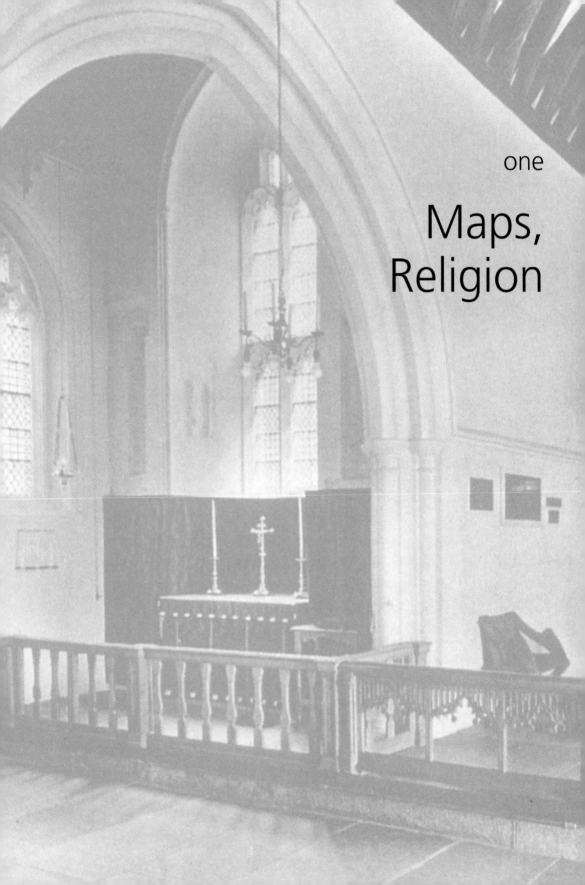

one

Maps, Religion

This copy of an Elizabethan map (late sixteenth century) showing defences of Penryn and Falmouth against Spanish shipping and raiding parties. The two castles each marked with a cross, Pendennis (right) and St Mawes (left), built by Henry VIII, guarded the entrance to the harbour with their cannons (quite a few cannon balls have been found at Blackrock halfway between the two). Not a lot can be seen of Falmouth at this time. Penryn can be seen (bottom right) with what is left of the Collegiate church and wooded lands nearby where three small ships (near the barriers) are chained together to stop Spanish and French fleets slipping into the town to burn, rape and pillage.

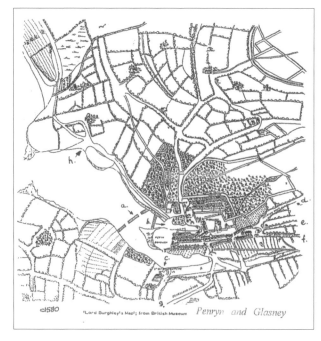

Penryn and Glasney

Lord Burghley's Map of Penryn and Glasney, c. 1580. The letter 'a' points to where the chain barriers were placed, a few hundred yards from the town and churches; 'b' towards Glasney and the Collegiate church of St Thomas which was built on a six-acre wooded site which included a deer park and orchards; 'c' towards the church of St Gluvias, consecrated 25 July 1318; 'd' would have been the Helston Road; 'e' points to West Street (as we know it) – it was also known as North Street, Pig Street and Calver Street; 'f' Truro Lane; 'g' towards Flushing and Mylor and 'h' the empty road to Falmouth.

Above right: 1815 map by E. Mogg of London showing the road the mail coach would have taken between Falmouth and beyond. Before the Penny Post was introduced by Roland Hill on 6 May 1840, all letters were charged a rate depending upon the distance they had to travel. The first Penryn postmistress was Eliza Rowe who had a salary of £72; a postman earned £18 5s. A local paper dated 1 October 1841 said that Mr F. Bice had been appointed to the position of postmaster when Miss Rowe resigned. The Penryn Post Office had at that time been under the management of the Rowe family for 150 years. It was situated in St Thomas's Street in 1823, moving to The Quay in 1830. Mail was carried by Messrs Rivers & Co. On leaving Falmouth, the coach would approach Penryn alongside the river, travel up St Thomas's Street where it would load up and then go up Market Street and down Truro Lane (Truro Lane is so steep at the top I believe the coach went down St Gluvias Street). From there it went up Truro Hill, probably stopping to pick up the mail of James Edwards at Bellevue, John Enys at Enys Estate and Sir William Lemon at the Carclew Estate. The first change of horses would be at the Norway Inn and then on to Truro and beyond. The mail would arrive in London a few days later. By 1873, Mary Jane Tamlyn was the postmistress; in 1836 the rail link to Falmouth opened. Sometime later the mail must have gone by rail leaving Penryn at 6.40 a.m. (with an extra stamp it left at 6.50 a.m.) and would arrive in London at 4 p.m. the same day.

MAIL COACH FALMOUTH & BEYOND

Published Feb.18th.1815 by E.Mogg.

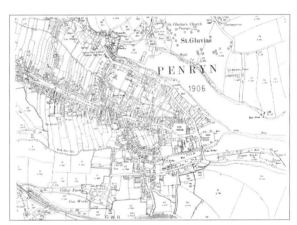

Below right: Penryn in 1906 and The Green is noticeable, standing just above The Quay and Custom House in a place where a row of houses was destroyed during the bombing of the town on 13 May 1941 when several bombs were dropped in Mill Lane and the Quay Hill area. Twenty-three houses, a shop and a Church institute were demolished resulting in eighteen deaths from a child as young as two years old to a seventy-eight-year-old. Many other houses in the area were damaged but the granite-built houses withstood the blasting. Near The Green is a memorial to those who lost their lives in the bombing raid. Following the main streets on each side it is possible to see how long the back gardens were.

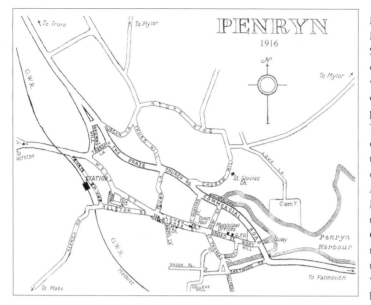

Map of Penryn 1916. The Municipal Offices in Broad Street are close to the post office where Miss Palmer was the post-office mistress, opening from 8 a.m. to 8 p.m. six days a week. Albert Tresidder was the caretaker of the combined post and telegraph office (telephone exchange), Benjamin Annear was the mayor with Matthew Henry Trescott town clerk, Charles Sidney Goldman was an MP. To the left of the map, next to the station, is marked 'private road' – this belonged to the GWR (Great Western Railway) and it had a locked gate at each end which was opened and closed each day by a GWR employee. The road was purchased by the council after the Second World War.

Harvest Festival at the Methodist chapel in Chapel Lane, 1889, taken by Harrison of Falmouth. The first reference to Wesleyan Methodism in Penryn was recorded in John Wesley's journal as, 'Tuesday, 27th September 1748 at one o'clock! at a convenient place surrounded by trees'. In 1755 evidence shows that there was a Methodist Society class meeting in a place at the back of Penryn main street. The many times John Wesley preached at Penryn was at least eleven times being recorded in his journal. He stayed mainly at the home of Mrs Rapson in Tresooth Lane. Minutes taken at a Methodist conference in 1788 indicate that a chapel was to be built in Penryn. The conveyance of a piece of land dated 30 September 1788 was from cordwainer Benjamin Moore of Penryn and painter Henry Pascoe of the now named Chapel Lane, Redruth. A Sunday school was started in 1812 by Miss Claire Truscott. Prior to this, services were held in a loft in a building at the bottom of New Street, demolished during the widening of Commercial Road in 1934. Extensions to the chapel were carried out in 1838 and 1847. On 25 January 1859, the first organ was installed; in 1888 a harmonium superseded the organ and was played by Mrs Sawyer and later by Mr William Hosken. Previously music was provided by a bass viola, a couple of flutes and on occasions a 'serpant'. Female singers in 1829 were paid 30s and male singers 20s but in 1853 an equal pay campaign was successful and £2 6s 6d was paid to both. In 1869 the chapel celebrated its first anniversary although sites were still being inspected for a new chapel.

The interior of the present chapel seated 450 people on the ground floor and another 400 in the gallery (the old chapel only seated 450). For special occasions 1,000 people could be provided with places. The building was designed by architect Mr Trounsan from Penzance and built by Carkeek of Redruth. John Freeman's granite firm of Penryn were responsible for the stone work and excluding the cost of the site the total building costs were just under £5,000. It was opened on 14 February 1893. Messrs Four Acre & Co. of Plymouth made the three-light stained-glass windows and Messrs Jackson & Son of London fashioned the plaster ceiling. Joel Blamey, the local bank manager, laid the large granite 'cup and ball' at the apex of the front façade. I well remember as a boy seeing Jack Truan, a mason who worked for Curtis, a local builder who did maintenance work on the building, lift and relay the heavy granite ball.

A service was held in the old chapel on the morning of the opening of the new building and was conducted by the Revd M. Westcomb followed by a public luncheon in the Temperance Hall. Special guests included the mayor of Penryn and civic leaders from Falmouth. In the afternoon the congregation saw the wonderful and imposing interior of the new building with its lovely plaster ceiling and heard Dr J.H. Rigg preach the first sermon which lasted almost an hour. It was a memorable occasion with the mayor and corporation of Penryn attending. There was also a band and choir under the leadership of Mr J.M. Thomas. Divine service was conducted in the evening by Mr G.J. Smith of Truro. Five days later on Sunday 19 February three baptism services were conducted. The first wedding took place on 27 February between choir members Darce Moore and Ernie Clemens. Seen here are a group of Wesleyans on an outing to Tremough, c. 1910.

Above, left and right: A rare postcard dated 1905 showing the present lychgate and the fifteenth-century tower of St Gluvias church which was restored by J.P. Aubyn in 1883 and characteristically Cornish, being built using granite and slate. On the gate's north wall a stone tells of a man's helplessness against storms and tempest and the tragedy of a transport ship. It's the last paragraph on the postcard that is of interest – 'Do you know that the Church on this cd [card] It was one of my first attempts with my camera – not a bad photo for me. N.K'. (He was so pleased with his efforts that he made the picture into a postcard). It was cancelled with a Penryn postmark at 12.30 p.m. on June or July 6 1905 with the number 608 which was allocated to the town's post office at that time.

St Gluvias church was built using local labour and granite and was consecrated by the Bishop of Exeter, Walter-de-Stapedon; it was rebuilt possibly on the same foundations many centuries later. This was the church that the Enys family attended regularly – could it be one of them in the photograph? Not far from where Church Road and The Causeway meet is a coach house where the carriage and horses were rested during the service. The photograph shows that the unsightly wall at the west end has been demolished and replaced with ornamental gates and railings. The lychgate has been moved further down the road, renovated and rebuilt, all for £60. A lower wall was built with an opening so that worshippers could park their cars behind.

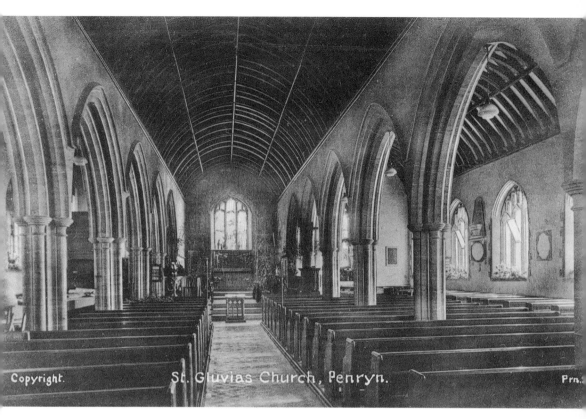

St. Gluvias Church, Penryn.

The interior of the beautifully constructed St Gluvias church with carved stone and wood. The gas lighting was removed and electric lighting installed during the alternations in the 1950s. The sun shines through the attractive stained-glass windows onto the high altar in the sanctuary; they were replaced after being removed during the Reformation. Beside the churches of St Gluvias and Glasney, the people of Penryn had a chapel of their own, the chapel of St Mary which stood in the middle of the street. It was built with £20 obtained from the sale of jewels, vestments and plate removed from St Gluvias church during the Reformation. The Town Hall and Market House stand on the old site. On a happier note from a local newspaper came these snippets:

Keep Waiting On The Turnpike

Howarde, the keeper of Treleaver-gate, near Penryn, was summoned … for detaining Mr. John Boeden, on the night of the 20th ult, fifteen minutes at the above gate. It being proved that Howarde had locked the gate and gone to bed, he was fined 1s. 6. and 18s. 6. costs

14 September 1838

Patience

Married on Wednesday week, at St. Gluvias, Mr. John Taylor, hind [estate manager] at Scorrier, to Miss Ann Tredwen, of Penryn, after a courtship of 22 years, during which time the bridegroom married two others.

25 December 1835

Above left: The inside of St Gluvias church, *c.* 1930. Apart from the Reformation few major alterations have taken place. During the Reformation many churches were stripped of their valuables and medieval glory and the destruction of priceless stained-glass windows. During the 1860s it was obvious that the churches were in dire need of restoration. This church was completed in 1883; the gas lighting had been removed and replaced with electric lighting during the alterations in the 1950s. Further changes were made by Sir Ninian Comper when the chancel was lowered to its original position, the whole church floored with slate headstones and the organ moved to the south-west corner. When John Sheepshanks was vicar (1824-1845) the following occurred and was written up by a local newspaper:

Sacrilegious Theft

Whereas William Niness, (son of William Niness, the younger), *alias* Young Cross, of the borough of Penryn in the county of Cornwall, brazier, stands charged with having broken into the parish church of St. Gluvias and Penryn, and sacrilegiously stolen therefrom five pieces of silver plate, and other articles, and has since absconded. We, the undersigned, do hereby offer a reward of ten guineas, to be paid to any person or persons who shall apprehend the said William Niness, and shall bring him before William Pender Roberts, Esq. one of his Majesty's Justices of the Peace for the said county of Cornwall, at Penryn aforesaid.

The said William Niness, is about 22 years of age, about 5 feet 6 inches high, rather stout made, has a heavy slouching walk, is of dark complexion, marked with the small-pox, black eyes with a downcast look, has an aquiline nose, and black hair, he generally wears an olive fustian short jacket and trowsers, has made one voyage to America, and has exhibited himself in this county and Devonshire on a mountebank stage. Any person after this notice discovered harbouring or concealing the said William Niness, will be prosecuted. Henry Rowe, churchwarden of St. Gluvias; Thomas Pearce, Thomas Rogers, churchwardens of Penryn.

19 October 1827

Above right: A reward of £20 was offered, three men were charged with robbery, what they had taken was never found. Replacements were purchased in 1828 for £41 9s and each article was marked 'Parish of St Gluvias and Borough of Penryn by voluntary subscriptions 1828'. This picture shows St Gluvias Chuch from the burial ground, *c.* 1900.

Because of death-watch beetle, dry rot and the ravages of time, the bells of St Gluvias church became too dangerous to ring. They were removed during the Second World War and sent to Taylors of Loughborough to be renovated. They were returned together with two newly cast treble bells. A generous donation by two families and a new steel frame given in memory of Charles Templeman enabled the peel to be enlarged to eight. Seen here are seven bells and workmen in 1948.

St Gluvias church was extremely lucky during the Second World War. As a child sheltering from an air raid at No. 83 The Terrace, my home in Penryn, I saw the parachute of a landmine come down behind the houses in the main street. It turned out that it had landed within a few hundred yards of the church without exploding (what a miracle!). Everyone nearby was evacuated and the bomb was dealt with by a Naval bomb disposal team on Sunday 7 September 1941. For the first time in the church's long history services were suspended for the day. Unfortunately during the same raid another land mine fell in the Glasney area and several people were killed. The 1948 photograph shows the eight bells and the inscription reads: 'This bell was given in thankfulness to God for the lives of Ernest Albert & Enid Amelia Webber by their 11 children'. Previously one was given by Mr and Mrs J.H. Tripp in 1948 'with thankfulness and love'. It wasn't usual to find a peel of eight bells but they were dedicated by Bishop Hunkin on 19 March 1949.

Above: Built of dressed granite and slate, the St Gluvias church vestry was enlarged in 1913, as it states on the engraved granite stone beneath the open window, 'To the glory of God and in memory of her brothers Francis Gilbert Enys and John Davies Enys. This Vestry was enlarged by Mary Ann Enys 1913'.

ON SUNDAY NEXT, 4th JUNE, 1882,

The Salvation Army

Will OPEN FIRE in the TOWN OF PENRYN

At half-past Two o'clock they will assemble in the Bowling Green and at Three o'clock in the Town Hall, (kindly lent by the Mayor,) Where the operations will be carried forward in real SALVATION ARMY STYLE.

At 6.30. the troops will again attack the enemy and the fighting will be kept up during the week.

The attack will be led by Aaron, Moses, and Happy Sarah.

Above: This appeared in the *Penryn Advertiser.*
Below: An advertisement from *The War Cry,* 15 June 1882:

OPENING OF PENRYN SALVATION ARMY

Bills have been posted throughout the town announcing the meeting on June 4th at 2.30 PM on Bowling Green a large plot of ground in the centre of the town, kindly granted to the Salvation Army by his Worship the Major for open air meetings and the Town Hall for the indoor meetings also by the same kind permission.

The meeting in the afternoon was attended by a quarter of the population of the town. A temporary stage has been put up for speakers by the well wishes of The Army. Perfect order prevailed throughout the day. The police did a good service with their presence. The most respectable of the town attended the afternoon meeting. The kindness and respect with which the people treated us reflects great credit on the town.

The meetings at night both in the open air and the Town Hall will never be forgotten. We had a procession through the principal streets to the Town Hall at night and there was also an orderly mock procession which reflected great credit on the so-called 'roughs'. We had ours in front. They elected a leader, and followed us singing the same hymn as we did and kept good time and the best order. We had great difficulty to get to the platform, the aisles of the Hall were so densely packed. We had not a quarter of the room necessary for the people who wanted to get in. May someone's heart be moved to help us in getting a place where we might put the people who are anxious to attend our meetings. The attack was led by Captain A. Hore, Ex-Captain Moses, 'Hallelujah Jim' the Champion War Cry seller and 'Happy Sarah' of Falmouth No. 1 assisted by a few kind Christians of other churches. We finished with the speaker after Christ, four of whom found what they sought and went home praising God. Who will help us get a place to carry on the fight? A large tent would be acceptable for the Summer.

Opposite below: The sextant of St Gluvias church, Tom Perkins, restored the old St Gluvias Cemetery chapel, built in 1872 by W.H. Bennett in memory of a former vicar of the church. The chapel became derelict several years ago but after £400 was spent on restoration it is now back in use. The photograph shows Owen Vincent on the left and Wally Treloweth, John Quintrell and Tom Perkins on the right, *c.* 1950.

Above left: The Penryn Salvation Army was formed and six months later mentioned in a local newspaper article, 'Our New Barracks', which was a little hall behind Edward's grocer shop at the top of Market Street. The photograph shows the door which leads down a path to the hall, a notice board above the door shows the times of the services. A Morris commercial vehicle is waiting to load or unload with the town clock in the fog in the distance, when this photograph was taken in the 1930s. When the Salvation Army was being formed in 1882, Penryn was well lit by gas, had an abundance of water, a well-established rail network, a national school for boys and girls, John Freeman's works employed a large number of men as did a paper mill, Tanyard, an engineering works, an iron foundry and a bone and manure works; life was getting better. Like so many towns at that time, whenever the Salvation Army were on parade, they were subjected to abuse and stoning (which is why the ladies had to wear their poke-bonnets). They carried on regardless of any setbacks, persevered and formed their own band within twelve months.

Above right: A week after being formed under Captain W. Weale and Lieutenant R. W. Bach on Saturday 9 June, the Salvation Army mustered their troops in the market place at 7 p.m. the grand march made their way to the barracks led by the big drum and fiddle to a rejoicing meeting at 8 p.m. The following morning, ammunition was served at 7 a.m. by the King and the town was bombarded by the muster from the barracks and was followed by an open-air demonstration on The Green at 11 a.m. They met again at 2 p.m. for a march and then went inside for a sharp shooting meeting led by the King's son. Terms of peace were read by the big gun at 6.30 p.m. when all sinners were asked to surrender at the salvation meeting. The next day at 3 p.m., after meeting at the barracks, a grand march took place starting at 4.30 p.m. to the field led by Captain Prosser and the Falmouth Brass Band together with a mounted officer, where a monster tea fight took place. After tea a Hosanna meeting on the field was led by Captains Weale, Prosser, Veal, Purnell and the soldiers. Children under the age of fourteen were admitted at half price and elders paid 9d for the tea.

The photograph on the postcard taken by Treloar, a Penryn photographer, are Captain Betty Manning and Lieutenant Alice Thorne stationed in Penryn around 1922.

(I contacted the Salvation Army for explanations of some of the terms used in the passage above. The 'King' was God, the 'King's Son' was Jesus and 'ammunition' was a word used for faith. The 'big gun' is a reference to God.)

A Penryn Salvation Army outing to Tremough in 1924 with the corps, friends and Captain Skinner and Lieutenant Field in charge. They came to Penryn in August 1923, taking over from Captain T. Large. A young Jimmy Driscoll is seen here with his mother near the Salvationist with a poke bonnet. Before Captain Skinner left Penryn in May 1925, the following was announced:

September 19th 1924

At Wednesday's evening meetings Captain Skinner announced that the target of £26 fixed by headquarters to be raised by the harvest festival of the Penryn corps has been attained. The ready response of the general public to appease, speaks well for the esteem and appreciation in which the Salvation Army is held and considering the scarcity of money and necessitous times, is highly satisfactory. The Captain extended a hearty vote of thanks to all who had in any way, either in gifts or by collecting, contributed to the success of the effort.

The Falmouth Salvation Army Band came to the cinema hall, Penryn on Sunday 20 March, 1935. The meeting was conducted by Major N. Narraway.

Captain Mary Pamela Sampson came to Penryn from St Just on 10 May 1934 and lived at No. 84 Market Street (just down the road from the hall). She had her marching orders on the 10 May 1935, giving her ten days to take over the corps at Keyhanm Devonport on 16 May. She married Captain Squibb at Belina in 1940; Captain R. Squibb was also at Penryn with Lieutenant Thompson in late 1935, living at Mutton Row.

Nora Hellard, a lovely woman known to everyone in Penryn. She was a Salvationist who, I believe, never wore uniform. She would do anyone a favour and ran errands for a few pence. Having had a hard life all her life, it was she that took me to a harvest festival at the Salvation Army (I lived opposite the hall with my family on The Terrace) as a three-year-old child. I couldn't explain to my mother afterwards what I had seen. I kept saying 'up on high' 'up on high'. Nora told my mother that I saw grapes hanging up. That was just before the start of the Second World War when the fruit became plentiful and my mother bought some; I have loved them ever since. Nora, seen here in 1935, lived with her relations (never marrying) in Helston Road and died in the 1970s.

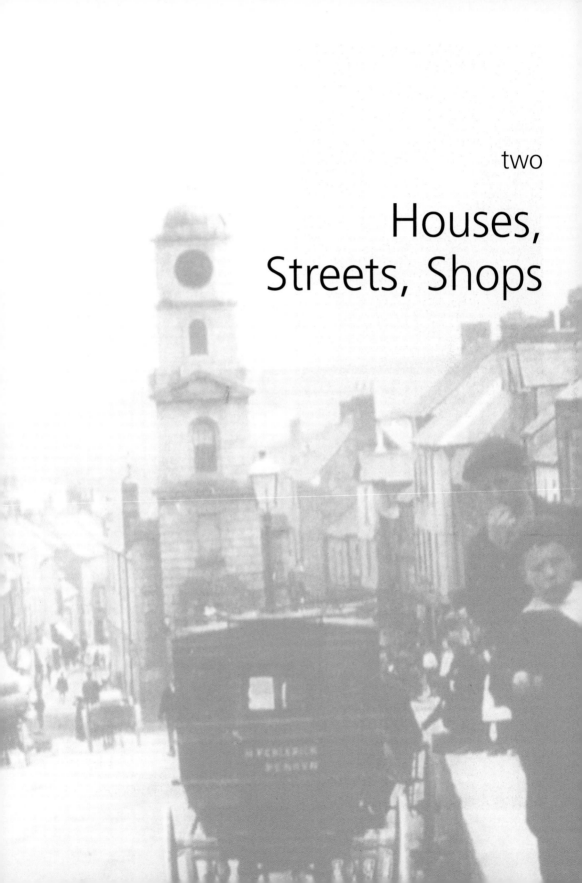

two

Houses,
Streets, Shops

Above left: The approach road to Carclew is nearly one mile long and approached through an avenue of lofty lime trees. It was here just after the Second World War that a most notable effort of land reclamation took place, making rapid progress in approximately ninety acres having already been planted with potatoes and oats. The land until quite recently formed part of the woodlands of Carclew which is within a few miles of Penryn. The work has been taken over by Mr Gill, a noted rhododendron specialist and horticulturist. He started by eradicating several hundred trees by means of a New Zealand tree puller. Some of the larger tree roots had to be dynamited. The thick bracken was cut and burned, providing potash for the soil and was ploughed in. Mr Gill was congratulated on the results so far obtained by the Duke of Norfolk who visited the estate with the Minister of Agriculture, Cedric Drive, and was thanked for a most valuable war effort at a time when the country was in such urgent need of them.

Above right: Portrait of Sir Charles Lemon by an unknown artist.

The front of the envelope sent and signed by Sir Charles Lemon to Tonbridge dated 25 January 1937 and franked by a crown cancellation. Being a MP he was entitled to free postage

Sir Charles Lemon allowed quite a number of functions to take place on his estate; in July 1827 there was a baby show. A Mr Davey charged mothers and guests 6d return to take them to the estate by horse and wagonette.

An engraving of 1823 by T. Jearons from a Stockdale drawing showing the magnificent Carclew House built near the top of a hill surrounded by trees and open parkland. The first owner was of one of ten known as 'the great' William Lemon who came from a Germoe family. His investments in the appropriately named Wheal Fortune enabled him to move to Truro and in 1739 he built a fine town house regarded as the best around in Princess Street. Other shrewd investments in Gwennap copper mines enabled him to branch out into commerce and banking. Ten years later he bought and completed the construction of Carclew House which had lain unfinished for twenty years. William Lemon laid out the estate into parkland and deer parks, marking his entry into the landed gentry.

Carclew House. In 1733 Lemon was elected an Alderman and became mayor of Truro in 1737. His signature then was written with obvious pride and he must have felt as though he had reached the summit of his ambition. He served a second time as mayor in 1750. The house he had built in Princess Street in Truro originally contained a chapel with an organ and a set of choral performers were hired for the services. He was such a lover of music he presented St Mary's church with an organ.

As stated in 1749 Mr William Lemon, the rich Truro mine owner and merchant, bought the Carclew estate from James Bonython. The house itself was partly built in 1728 from plans drawn up by William Edwards, a self-educated architect for Samuel Kemp of Penryn who had married the daughter and heiress of Richard Bonython after his death his wife bequeathed it to James Bonython.

In 1760 his grandson, later Sir William Lemon, inherited the estate. He was succeeded by his second son, Sir Charles Lemon in 1824. The late nineteenth century saw the end of the Lemon line. A nephew of Sir Charles, Colonel Arthur Tremayne, although surviving the charge of the Light Brigade at Balaclava during the Crimean War was badly wounded and he himself was succeeded upon his death by his son, Captain William Tremayne, in 1905.

Above left: This elegant house with its large columned entrance and broad staircase had seven bedrooms. The staircase is made out of beautiful wrought iron with a hardwood hand rail. Notice the huge fluted columns and nicely formed plastered ceiling with what could be an electric light hanging from the centre. The two windows without curtains allow daylight in at the turn of the stairs. Tongue and grooved flooring is partly covered by a carpet dropping to the floor below. On both sides of the staircase places have been designed where family portraits could be displayed. The exterior of the building had a noble appearance that opened on to a lawn and drive of tall lime trees. The west front overlooked a wooded valley surrounded by distant hills. Tragedy struck in the early hours on 5 April 1934 when a fire mysteriously broke out and quickly spread. William Tremayne, his family, guests and servants escaped in their night clothes and watched on the lawn as the fire took hold. With the fire destroying the telephone wires, the chauffeur had to drive to Penryn and Falmouth to summon the fire brigades. However even with help from these two fire brigades plus the Truro brigade, the house could not be saved from total destruction. The county had truly lost a magnificent property.

It is interesting to note that three members of the Lemon family served as MPs for the borough of Penryn – William (1770-1774); Charles (1807-1812) and Sir William in 1830.

Above right: The Enys family tree can be traced back to at least 1272 when a certain Robert-de-Enys was the first member of the family recorded in the college of arms long before the coat of arms was designed in the 1800s. The manor was recognised by the Bishop of Exeter as a freehold estate. The name Enys is an ancient Celtic name meaning 'clearing in the forest'. In a clearing in the reign of Edward I, a short distance to the north of Penryn, the Enys family built the original house in the shape of a letter 'E' (see my last book *Around Penryn*). The old Tudor mansion dating from around the end of the sixteenth century burned down in 1826 after which another house for the Enys family was built in 1830. The building costs were about £6,500 and to ensure that should there ever be another fire, there would be a sufficient supply of water, some freshwater lakes and reservoirs were constructed on the estate.

Right: Enys Estate is noted for its lovely walks throughout the entire estate as depicted in this postcard posted in the summer of 1920. The huge beech trees pass the well-stocked freshwater lakes. With the large deer park, venison, pheasant, rabbits and fish were often on the menu. Poaching was not uncommon.

Below: Enys House, built in 1830 of handsome silver-grey granite stone from local quarries, was designed in a similar architectural style as so many Cornish houses of that period. Rebuilt by George Samuel Enys (the owner at that time) on the foundations of the old house. The view is taken from the side of the house and a tall tropical plant named a 'yucca' can be seen. The three men standing nearby could be members of the Eyes family or perhaps one could be the gardener proudly showing off this exotic plant. The croquet lawn dates to around 1900.

At the beginning of the fifteenth century the word 'de' in 'de Enys' lapsed and the family was simply named Enys or Enys of Penryn. In 1660 Samuel Enys was MP for Penryn at the first parliament of Charles II.

Above: The early 1900s and to the side of the house summer house has been added. The tropical plant has been replaced by palm trees and there is a different layout of the shrubs next to the gravel path. In the 1600s the Enys began to have trouble with their affairs which more than once saw them sell or mortgage off pieces of land – Samuel Enys gambled at cards, cock fighting and dice and lost more than he ever won. So much so that by the eve of the civil war the family seemed to be on the point of disappearing from the ranks of the local gentry.

Below: The croquet lawn, plants and shrubs have been replaced by what was possibly a fete. Although the postcard was not despatched, it is signed by Sarah L. Enys and dates to around the early 1920s. The crowd of people appear to be enjoying themselves – could this have been a Sunday school outing? Perhaps the sailors were from the cadet sailing ship *Foynhaven* which often sailed into Penryn for regattas etc. The Dutch Navy were stationed here during the war.

In 1627 sixteen-year-old Samwell Enys left for Spain, staying in San Sebastian; when he returned in 1646 the Civil War was not over. He paid stiff fines because his family's Royalist attitude did not affect him because whilst abroad he had become a wealthy merchant.

Right: Enys House clock tower, built from local granite, reached from a staircase for ease of winding! Samwell married Elizabeth Pendarves of Roscrow in 1647 whose father possessed a large amount of land. On the death of his father, Samwell bought back what remained of the Enys Estate from his brother, Thomas, also land that his father had been forced to sell earlier. He redeemed mortgaged land and became a successful ship owner carrying out business with Spain and Portugal, investing in tin mines and trading in commodities including tin. The family were back on their feet again. Samwell died in 1698, aged eighty-nine.

His grandson, Samwell, was now addressed as Samuel. In 1709 he became the sheriff of Cornwall and in the same year he married Dorothy, sister and co-heiress of Sir William Willys Bart who died in 1744.

Samuel's eldest son John became sheriff of Cornwall in 1751 and married Lucy, daughter of Francis Bassett Esq. of Tehidy and the aunt of Lord DeDunstanville. He became sheriff again in 1796 and died on October 11, 1802. The male line had continued for five centuries until 1802 when John Enys died without an heir and his sister Lucy Anne inherited the estate.

Below: The front of the house in 1920. Lucy Anne Enys inherited the property in 1802 from her childless brother who at the time was the widow of Samuel Hunt. The *Royal Sign Manual* of 27 December 1813 states, 'she and her family were authorised to assume the name of Enys only' (in place of Hunt). At the time of the fire in 1826, Lucy Anne's son, John Samuel Enys, had two sons, Francis Gilbert and John Davies. They travelled to Patagonia and New Zealand and brought back numerous exotic plants and seeds, including the yucca mentioned earlier, enhancing the property for many years. At the death of his unmarried brother, Francis John Davies inherited the property but since then the name Enys has not continued in that male line.

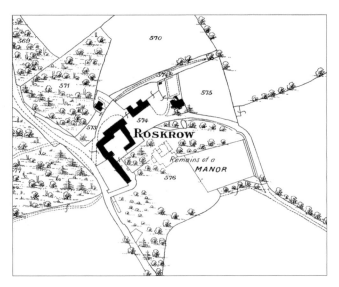

Above: Roskrow House is situated near Treluswell on the Helston Road and enjoys wonderful panoramic views overlooking Penryn and onwards to St Anthony Lighthouse. There is evidence an old manor house existed here dating back to the Domesday Book. It was built for the Roskrow family whose name became extinct in the male line in the reign of Henry VI (1442-1461). Thomas Harry became the next owner during the reign of Henry VIII and he took the name of Roskrow. In 1641 his grandson sold the barton to Samuel Pendarvis and it continued to be his family's seat until 1725. Alexander Pendarvis was MP for Penryn seven times; his first wife Dorothy De-Burgh bore him no heir. He later married Mary Granville when she was only seventeen years of age but it was an unhappy marriage and when he died in 1723, she moved to London.

The next owner is believed to have been Francis Bassett, a major land-owning family in the county. Francis passed on the estate to Lord De-Dustanville. Later the house was occupied by the Fox family and subsequently William Yates, one-time owner of the thriving Ponsanooth woollen manufactory. It fell into disrepair and was doomed to be levelled in the 1890s.

The map shows the new Roskrow and also the remains of the old manor which was taken from a catalogue of houses and land which were to be sold on 31 July 1906 at the King's Arms Hotel, Penryn, by Andrews & Sons, Plymouth.

During the wars with France and Spain in the eighteenth century, many prisoners were interned at both Roskrow and Kergilliak.

Unusual postcard by Opie of Redruth picturing the Tudor-style manor house similar to the one standing today but without the decorative wood. There are records of bitter complaints about the poor accommodation, food and water supplies made by French privateers on their return to France who had been kept at Roskrow where officers and men were herded together. Fish had formed a large part of the prisoners' diet and there was particular grievance about the quality of boots and shoes provided for them.

Postcard by Opie showing beautifully laid-out lawns. There was also a large full-size tennis court on the north-east side of the manor. Between April 1737 and June 1795 at least 600 prisoners of war including 500 Frenchmen from the camps at Roskrow and Kergilliak were buried in St Gluvias Churchyard. However some French prisoners did get liberty and one, John David, married Elizabeth Mitchell of Penryn on 28 April 1762.

Opposite below: The approach road to Roskrow, a few hundred yards from the main road. The French prisoners confined to the Penryn district were extremely industrious and skilful in making an astonishing variety of articles from wood and bone with primitive tools. Some of the workmanship showed exceptional artistry and skill. The articles sold for high prices and many are no doubt still in existence.

Above: West Hill House, 1910. Built on the site of a cottage in 1780, it was extended in 1800. In 1898 the house was owned by auctioneer, valuer and estate agent, Mr B. Dingle.

The people shown on this postcard are Mr William Kneebone, a teacher, his wife Elizabeth, their daughter Effie, also a teacher and Effie's daughter.

Below: The house on The Causeway owned by Hobson Dyer before 1791 became derelict and Trenowth House was built on the site. It was constructed by William Pellow from local granite and in parts faced with limestone plaster.

It was close to the house where a landmine landed unexploded in September 1941. Looking at the postcard, St Gluvias church is to the right behind the house. I don't know the men's names but the dog's name is Rover!

Right: The Michells rented Trenowth House from William Campbell, who lived in Canada. The advert shows that the house became a boarding and day school for young ladies which was run by the Misses Michells from at least 1867. By 1880 they purchased the house and taught mathematical and commercial studies. After teaching for more than fifty years, Miss Michell died in 1923. The house was sold in the April of that year for £620.

Trenoweth House, Penryn.

BOARDING AND DAY SCHOOL FOR YOUNG LADIES.

THE MISSES MICHELL

Will resume the duties of their Establishment, (D.V.)

On Monday, January 23rd, 1882.

Below: Tremough was listed in the Domesday Book of 1086 as being in the district of Treliver or Trelever as it is known today. This beautiful Georgian house was built by Penryn merchant John Worth in 1703 but its origins are believed date to the late thirteen or early fourteenth centuries when it was owned by the Blois and Tremough families. It was built of granite, with mahogany and oak panelling, beatiful staircases and moulded plaster ceilings.

After John's demise his son inherited the mansion but due to his extravagant lifestyle he mortgaged it for £6,000 in 1737. By 1775 the Worth family lost possession of the house when it was sold to Robert Crow. *The West Briton* reported in 1827 that Tremough Barton, a 137-acre, ancient stone-fronted mansion in a dilapidated state was to be auctioned; it was bought by a John Tilley. Benjamin Samson was the owner in 1858 followed by William Shilson, his son Henry Shilson and Col. Louis Faulkner-Brown. In July 1919 the clock tower's stables were destroyed by a massive fire, it being reported that Penryn Fire Brigade took so long to catch and harness a pair of horses to pull the water wagon that they arrived too late. The Penryn fire brigade manhandled the engine and ladder cart.

Tremough was auctioned in 1926 by Boswell & Co. at the Red Lion, Truro and bought by Col. Mountford-Longfield who had been renting the house since 1924. Nineteen years later he sold the house to an order of nuns 'Les Filles de la Croix' who ran the building as a convent to, 'raise the standard of girls' education'. In 1999 Tremough was bought by the Falmouth School of Arts and became the hub of the Cornish University. As so many years ago, Penryn is once again the centre of learning – for good or bad I can't make up my mind.

Above: In March 1930 at a Penryn Town Council meeting it was reported that the Minister of Health approved the proposal to erect fifty-four houses in Penryn. An offer of £300 was made to Mr H. Thomas for land at Glen View as well as £375 to Miss Gill for land at Green Lane. Should these offers not be accepted the council would seek compulsory powers to acquire the land. At the next council meeting it was agreed to purchase land at Glen View for building purposes from Mr H. Thomas for £350. In view of difficulty in obtaining building land at Green Lane, it was agreed the district valuer should value land adjoining the Glen View site belonging to Mr F. Chegwidden with a view to purchasing. It was reported later that the district valuer had valued the land at Glen View at £280; Mr Chegwidden had accepted the council offer to purchase at that sum. Tenders were advertised to build the houses and one was accepted. For the erection of thirty-one houses at Glen View the tender of T.B. Rundle of Padstow of £12,975 was accepted. The tenders of Percy Williams of Stithians of £6,800 for erecting seventeen houses opposite Glen View and £800 for erecting two houses at The Praze were also accepted. The photograph for the postcard was taken outside No. 5 Glen View around 1932 and it appears the milkman is on his delivery with his copper measures and horse-drawn cart. The old buildings and gates have been renewed, the old ones probably going for the war effort. It's now a lot busier with cars and children.

T.H. Treloar was the publisher of this postcard at West End, where at the far left of these large houses the triumphal arch was erected (see last picture). Today the fences and gate post are still there, the road past these houses turned down to pass Trelawney Park on to the main road to Redruth and Truro.

Advancing a number of years on from the last picture, this shows West End a little further on. The man is proudly showing off his pony whilst two boys wait for the photographer to set up his camera. The houses are still the same today with no garden to the front but longer ones at the rear. On the right behind the foliage is West Hill House.

Opposite below: To celebrate the Diamond Jubilee of Queen Victoria, this triumphal arch of flowers, bunting and foliage was erected at the West End. The banner reads: '1837 GOD SAVE THE QUEEN 1897'. The ladies on the extreme left do not have funny hats on; they are the gate posts to the houses (see the top of this page).

Another Treloar postcard showing the end of West Street and the beginning of West End, Mrs Thomas's fish restaurant being the striped shop in the middle background. Mutton Row is to the left near the fish shop where opposite, my grandparents had a small grocers' shop at No. 88 West Street at the turn of the last century. This could be near this date as the ladies are wearing long dresses of that period. There is no traffic in sight, not even a pennyfarthing!

FOR THE BEST QUALITY

Fish, Peas, Fish and Fritters

Guaranteed Fried only in Pure Beef Dripping.

No other Mixture whatever.

 GIVE ME A TRIAL.

Mrs. Thomas, THE FISH RESTAURANT,

WEST END, PENRYN.

OPEN AT 4.30 EVERY EVENING.

Mr Thomas's advertisement was placed in the local newspaper in 1930. The family business must have been going for quite a long time because I can remember as a young boy in the mid-1940s seeing a young Mr Thomas cooking his fish and chips using a coal fire.

Above left: Almost from the same point where the photograph of West Street was taken is the Co-Operative Society shop. In October 1920 a public meeting was called in the Town Hall by the Penryn Trades and Labours Council and Labour Party supported by Fred Richards and other councillors. It was thought that the time had come when a Co-Operative shop should be opened in Penryn, On 4 February 1921, recorded shareholders were to fill in the circulars and return them the next day. A free film show was organised at the Penryn Cinema in March to show the residents of Penryn how the Co-Operative Society operated. It took two years to organise circulars, a milk round and a free film show. The Co-Op opened sometime later because my family joined and always looked forward to the Christmas dividend; my mother's Co-Op number was 2822 which I knew because I ran the errands. The four ladies in the photograph worked at the shop. Back row, left to right: Phyllis Poat, Mary Rich (manageress). Front row, left Valerie Collins and right Heather Moore.

Above right: Taken around 1930 Fred Belbin's bread, confectionary shop and restaurant was well known for its delicious produce. The bake house was down Truro Lane beside the shop. My family lived on The Terrace almost opposite the shop and well remember buying hot splits at three for 1d, and my brother would sometimes eat a roast meal in the cafe/restaurant. Mr Belbin's first shop was situated on The Terrace near to Chapel Lane and the Seven Stars pub in 1910. He then moved to a cottage at No. 2 West Street which he demolished and built a shop and cafe on the site around 1912. Using an American Chevrolet van, Fred would deliver his produce to most of the outlying villages around Penryn. A very kind man, it was not uncommon to see Fred give his loose change to down-and-outs; he was also a very good sportsman (see later chapter). Standing in the doorway on the right is Fred's wife Mabel and on the left is Vera their daughter. Fred died in 1957 and the business was carried on by Phyllis the youngest daughter. Mabel died in 1965 and the business finally closed in the early 1970s.

Published by F. Chegwidden, this postcard dating to around 1910 has been taken halfway down Truro Lane where the leat would run down to St Gluvias Street from the spring at Treluswell a few miles away. At the top of this lane Fred Belbin ran his bread shop. Years before, the horse-drawn mail coach would race down to the bottom of the street, pass the Cross Keys public house on the right and then up Truro Hill opposite and away to the large estates beyond. The postcard was sent by the youth leaning on the gate and the young boy with the jug was called Jack (written on the back of the postcard). Notice the huge wheels on the horse-drawn cart on the left.

The Cross Keys at the bottom of Truro Lane, c. 1900. The licensee was a Charlotte Edwards, reputed to be a hard landlady. The lady standing in the doorway could be her waiting as well as the boys for the photographer to snap their picture.

The Praze (Cornish word for meadow), opposite the Cross Keys, *c.* 1912. Next to the lady wearing the long white dress is Truro Hill leading to Enys and on to the Carclew Estate. The road looks more like a dirt track rather than a busy commercial road that leads to St Gluvias church and the Quays before it reaches Falmouth.

Commercial Road leading to the Praze with the Cross Keys on the left at the bottom of Truro Lane, *c.* 1910. The picture shows No. 1 The Praze; the end house on the left was Dickie Dunstan's blacksmith shop. On the left of the photograph is a fast flowing stream which has been known to flood during heavy rain.

Left: Further down The Praze leading to the Sanitary Steam Laundry on the left, *c.* 1910. Richard Dunstan's blacksmith shop is on the left (see later chapter). Mrs Emily Davies' grocer shop is on the left. Next to the line of boys is granite merchant William Hosken's covered wagon – he had his depot in Commerical Road. By the state of the muddy road perhaps it has just rained.

Below: John Russell Edwards (known as J.R.) with his wife Mary in the doorway of their grocer shop at No. 94 Market Street in the 1950s. They moved there during the Second World War and took over the sub-post office from Mr Renfree who had been there a considerable time before hostilities began. Living on the terrace opposite I remember the couple and their son Michael very well. After the war and the lifting of restrictions, they sold Eldorado ice cream – tasting it for the first time at 2d each was wonderful. To the right of the family is the entrance to the Salvation Army and to the left of the window is the door to their home. They retired from business in 1968.

What a lovely picture taken around 1902 of a little well looked after donkey and cart standing in the main street alongside The Terrace. Could the well-dressed lady be Mrs James Hodgemoon, a general dealer from Broad Street? Perhaps it is Mrs Amelia Hooking or Miss Lucy Jennings, who were shopkeepers on The Terrace at that period of time.

Believed to be Mrs Ethelinda Ninness's grocer and sweet shop at No. 81 The Terrace around 1902. Fry's Chocolate is prominent. I lived with my family next door to the right and when I was growing up in the 1940s Mrs Lorrimoore and her daughter owned the shop. In the 1920s the cottage next door was demolished to make a front entrance to the Council School. Passing the next three cottages (I remember one having a bow window in the 1940s) is the Seven Stars public house, Robert Brokenshire being mine host at the time. Behind the roof of that establishment can be seen the tapered front of the Wesleyan chapel.

Above left: The heavy snowfall of 1947 lasted quite some time. This is Helston Road with the town clock in the background. The Bassetts, a well-known Cornish mining family, built the houses on the right and then rented them out for a small amount. Cattle were driven down the street on their way to the slaughterhouses and for years steel rings could be seen where the animals were tied up to the wall alongside The Terrace.

Above right: Penrick's horse-drawn omnibus ran daily to Falmouth with the last one leaving Falmouth at 10 p.m. This photograph of around 1900 shows the main street with the youngsters posing for the photographer alongside The Terrace. Beneath the black-faced town clock with a blanked-out window is the Town Hall and Magistrates' Court. From the local paper in 1840 the following was reported:

> On Monday evening last, three men in a pitiable state of destitution were taken into custody at Falmouth, for breaking a pane of glass in a shop window. They were taken before the magistrates, but the charge against them was withdrawn. In answer to enquiries by the mayor, they said their names were John Jamieson of Dumfries, Thomas Brown of Glasgow and Thomas Williams of Bridgwater. They were all habited in dresses made from old sacking stuff, which they said had been supplied to them by the magistrates at Penryn. They had no hats, stockings or shoes, and had not a penny amongst them. The mayor said they must be relieved, and as the board was sitting at Penryn, he sent them to the relieving officer there.

2 March 1840

Opposite below: With the trees in full leaf, the white face of the town clock shows 2.10 p.m. The postcard probably dates to between 1910-1912. On the left with the sunblind extended is the tailor and draper's shop of Mr Moon & Son. Further down the road on the left is St Gluvias Street. To the right, Edwin Dunnithorne had his shop near to the Red Lion public house where Henry Legassick was the landlord. The pub was frequented by the Penryn Freemasons until 1838 (The Masonic symbols are still above the doorways). One of the small shops could be that of grocer and draper Ernest Coade who is advertising clothes dying. The horse-drawn carriages are waiting for business outside the Wesleyan chapel. The house and shops behind were demolished in 1954 to make way for Saracen Place. Who is selling Pratt's Petroleum Spirit next to Moon's the outfitters? There is an enamelled sign above the shop – could it be the Penryn Hardware Stores who were ironmongers?

Above: Two types of horse power around 1903, the large one on the left could be a delivery round from many of the large shops, or with only three letters on the side of the wagon, could it be GWR? On the other side of the road small ponies and traps. The gentleman standing on the right may be outside a butcher's shop as there is something that looks like a huge piece of meat hanging outside the window. Further down the street the extended awning points to a summer's day. The entrance to the Magistrates' Court is through the doorway beneath the Clock Tower. The local paper reported the following in April 1898:

TO COURT IN A SACK

A woman named Sarah Maunder, summoned for cruelty to her children, failed to appear at Falmouth police-court on Wednesday. Mr. W. Jenkin, N.S.P.C.C., asked for a warrant. He did not know whether the woman was in a state of nudity, but he heard that the reason for her non-appearance was that she had nothing to wear. The Clerk said the Court could not provide her with clothes. Mr. Jenkin understood that at Penryn a man in a somewhat similar predicament was furnished with a sack. They were more civilised at Penryn [something I've know for a long time!]. The warrant was granted.

11 April 1898

Taken around the same period as the previous photograph, the clock has moved on to 4.15 p.m. The horse-drawn carriage awaits hiring and the children wait patiently for the photographer to take their picture. The enamelled Pratt's sign is still there over a shop that appears to sell galvanised items. Next door was the Elephant & Castle Hotel, one of the borough's principle hostelries, advertised in the *Penryn Advertiser* as a 'Posting Establishment'.

Sent to Holland in September 1927, this postcard shows the Penryn & Falmouth Motor Co. bus about to leave for Falmouth and running five minutes late. It should leave every half an hour and on the hour. The bus carries a Cornish number RL109? Coming up the street is a model 'T' Ford with electric lighting of around the same period. Although made in America, it has a right-hand drive. Henry Ford was famous for saying, 'you can have any colour as long as it's black'. Samuel Ruberry's stationary shop is on the left next to Mainwaring the grocer. On the right is the Weslyan chapel with electric lamps at the entrance.

Penryn, Broad Street looking South.

Above: Penryn main street in the 1940s. The photographer could well have taken this photograph from near the Seven Stars. On the right outside the Methodist chapel is a Hackney carriage stand. Austin and Morris cars and lorries can park easily with no sleeping policemen, yellow lines or traffic wardens. The Morris commercial stands outside Harry Mainwaring's grocer shop whilst the lady on the right with the children is about to pass Jas Pollard's butcher shop. Don't believe everything you read – it's not Broad Street but Market Street (the main street).

Right: A rather unusual photograph taken from the Clock Tower through the Penryn clock face by a steeplejack nearly sixty years ago. Looking towards Falmouth down the Penryn River, the one-way system is very narrow on both sides of the Town Hall and council offices and it appears that no yellow lines are in place yet.

Dating from around 1910, this postcard shows the lower side of the town clock with William Easom's shop on the right. He not only sold tobacco; he was a motorcar and motorcycle agent as well as selling bicycles. It looks as though the traffic could drive both ways with the horse and cart standing outside his shop and another making its way towards them – there wasn't a one-way system in operation. The Penryn bakery is next door and then came Mallett & Sons (the Truro firm). Next down is believed to be the original King's Arms public house. Behind the horse and cart (middle background) with a pillared entrance is the King's Arms after it moved to its present site. With two bicycles, one with a chain guard, leaning against the tree in full bloom, it must have been summer when this scene was snapped.

Mallet & Son opened in Penryn in Market Street around 1896 and sold just about everything from tools, house furnishings, lawn mowers and brass beds to cycling accessories including sunbeam, quadrants (four-wheel cycles) or any other make supplied at the lowest prices possible. Even perambulators and mail cars as needed. Look at the two lovely lanterns outside. The shop closed on 30 September 1909. On the reverse of the postcard sent from Truro to Camelford with a 1/2d stamp dated 5.30 p.m., 1 October 1909 it says, 'Dear Mother. This is our shop at Penryn which was closed yesterday. From Fay'.

Next to the Borough Hairdressers is George Leonard Hutt the chemist. The cafe and tea rooms next door belonged to Mr Jack Tripp who was the brother of Mabel Belbin; he worked for Fred Belbin the baker in West Street to learn the trade. When he left Belbin's he set up in competition (I don't think Belbin was very pleased). He then sold the business to Triggs. In the background is the King's Arms Hotel and public house. The Comer lorry could be on a delivery or moving up to the town centre. It was most unusual to see an Austin car, right, pulling a trailer when this photograph was taken in the 1950s.

Believed to be Edwin Thomas & Sons who were family butchers in Market Street, the shop has been decorated to celebrate the coronation of Edward VII in 1902. Today the health & safety inspectors would have a field day with carcasses hanging outside in the open. Also decorated next door could be the shop of a watchmaker but is it Nicholas Thomas or John Marshall Thomas?

Left: Copied from the *Penryn Advertiser*, this is also a copy drawing of the Mallett's postcard and it states the Penryn General Furnishing & Hardware Co. (late Mallett & Son) is now taken on by Chegwidden in 1910 in Market Street near Fish Cross.

Below: Penryn in 1890, taken at Fish Cross. On the right is the grocer shop of James Martin, who was also an agent for W. & A. Gilbey, Wine & Spirit Merchants, with the James Dole Wiltshire Bacon sign in the window. The road alongside is the top of New Street, opposite is St Thomas Street. A gentleman with a beard and top hat along with other well-dressed bearded gentlemen all wearing bowler hats, waits patiently for the photograph to be taken. There seem to be quite a number of people around and no traffic in sight.

Opposite: James Martin's shop on the corner of Market Street and New Street has now changed to Thomas Brimacombe and still sells Gilbey's wine and spirits; an extra sign for Sunlight Soap is in the window and next door is Frederick Chegwidden's newspaper shop. Further up the street on the same side there is a sign for Kodak on the chemist shop of Wilmar & Hocking. Further up is the cinema where Victor Rodrick was the proprietor in the Temperance Hall. The bus of the Penryn & Falmouth Motor Co. makes its way towards the Town Hall, with a registration number AF 9211, the other vehicle is a horse and cart making its way towards the crowd of people where everyone wears a hat of some type. Opposite is St Thomas Street and the shop of Mrs Mary Jewell selling groceries and Fry's chocolate when this postcard was produced around 1915. (The picture was used for the cover of *Around Penryn*).

Above: Lower Market Street around 1910. The two men and a boy on the left are outside Mrs James's outfitters and drapers shop, above are the Penryn Constitutional Club rooms where Ernest Webber was secretary and next door is the cycle shop of Will J. Easom who also had a depot on The Quay advertising Triumph cycles. Next door could be Ernest Coade, a grocer and draper with clothes on view in the window. Between the last shop and the bow-windowed shop of Edwin Dunnithorne, seedsman and market gardener is the Capital & Countries Bank Ltd with Charles Rule as manager. A Triumph cycle with a guard leans against a tree. On the right a pony and cart stands outside Ernest Knowle's 'The People's Butcher' shop. Just down from the Temperance Hall, after a few shops including Henry James Davies a boot and shoe dealer, is the old Golden Lion, then Thomas Hellings, and further down another cycle dealer James Eddy. According to the enamel sign he sold Arial cycles and motorcars as well as BSA bicycles and Price's lubricant. On the extreme right is the chemist of Wilmer & Hocking. Two boys are making their deliveries with hand trolleys.

Above: AF 6296 is the registration number on the car outside the watchmaker of Mr Thomas in Market Street in 1917. The two horses are pulling the cart towards the photographer standing on Fish Cross. A motorcycle with smaller horse power is parked outside William Easom's shop on the left, with the white-faced clock showing 1.45 p.m. and a worker sweeping up the leaves next to the Town Hall. The Weslyan chapel is just visible far left and the Temperance Hall to the far right which was built in the 1850s. Opposite the car is the stationer and printer of the *Penryn & Falmouth Advertiser*, Frederick Chegwidden who had his finger in more than one pie in Penryn.

Below: Benjamin William Curgenven & Son Stores in St Thomas Street, *c.* 1915. In 1897 the shop was known as the Penryn Supply Stores and was owned by Henry Liddicoat & Co. grocer & wine and spirit merchants. Liddicoat had been the manager of the shop since 1885 and bought it late in the 1890s; he was mayor of Penryn in 1892. The council in that year had plates made with the mayor's name on them to celebrate the coronation of Edward VII. After he died, his son Henry took over followed by Roy, his grandson, who ran the business. Roy was an officer in the Penryn Fire Brigade, dying in 1972. His son Peter carried on until the 1980s when the business was closed. So ended a family business for almost 100 years.

Above: Broad Street from Fish Cross, the former fish market which, in 1894, the *Penryn Advertiser* reported that the council was about to demolish because its revenue was almost nil. Behind the group of people is the pillared entrance to the King's Arms when John Pellow was landlord in the 1830s. In 1872, it became known as George Champion King's Arms Family and Commercial Hotel, Wine & Spirit Merchant, Maltster & Hop Merchant. Its telephone number was No. 3. The horse and carriage is waiting to be hired with the candle lamps attached and next door is the Supply Stores of Robert Furneax on his delivery round with the other horse and cart.

Right: There was a John Furneax, grocer and provision dealer in Broad Street in 1873. It this postcard dates from before 1910, the gentleman with the moustache would be aged approximately thirty-three. Within 100 yards there were quite a few grocers making a living. The window is full of the produce he sells – Fry's pure cocoa, boxes of fruit, tea, bread and so on with a lamp in each window and a lantern outside – perhaps he kept open late.

Broad Street looking towards Market Street. The car on the right is a two-door Model Y 8HP Ford with easy-clean wheels, built in 1938, and stands outside the supply store of Robert Leslie Furneax, the same family as the last postcard. The King's Arms is fully licensed with public and lounge bars selling Devonish beers and outside is a 1949 Sunbeam Talbot and extreme left a 1939 Vauxhall 10HP. It has been established the King's Arms did a flourishing trade as a coaching inn as far back as at least 1730. Like so many inns it has a ghostly past. Landlords have been touched on the shoulder with no one in sight, lights go on and off and one visitor got out of bed thinking there was a burglar and fell over a drawer full of clothes that neither he nor his wife had left there. Going towards where he thought there should be a door, he was astonished to find a blank wall. He awoke in the morning and the drawer full of clothes was still there. All the ghosts appear to be friendly.

The steps on the left of the picture belong to the three-storey house that was once the home of a packet ship's captain.

In 1830 the post office was situated on The Quay with Eliza Rowe the postmistress before it moved to the High Street and ? Francis Bice was postmaster in 1841. Miss Mary Jane Tamlyn became the postmistress in 1873 when it moved to Broad Street. This picture dates to around 1902 and shows the pillared entrance to the post office, money order, telegraph office and savings bank when Miss Mary Ann Southwood was in charge. Looking towards Fish Cross a number of Penryn's private schools were based here. Miss Edith Hill ran a propriety school and Miss Julia Dodd had a ladies' school. It then belonged to two doctors, Austen Bearne, a surgeon, James Blamey, also a surgeon and medical officer for the district. Could the draper's shop next door to the post office be Harry Lavine's? The hand-cart being pulled looks huge!

It is easy to date this postcard as the new post office was opened in July 1905. A building inspector would have a field day looking at the state of the scaffolding. Notice the workmen do not have hard hats. On the left is the barber's pole of young Fred Harris, tobacconist and hairdresser, whilst a young man on the left has completed his delivery with an empty basket.

The Square at the end of Broad Street, a few yards away from the Swan Inn, the Anchor Hotel and uphill from the quays. The large houses belong to some of the gentry of the borough – the town clerk to Penryn, Harbour and School Attendance Committee, George Appleby Jenkins, Major Norman Grey, borough treasurer Richard Hosken and Revd Frederick Woofenden (Wesleyan Methodist) etc. A few of these houses and the larger ones in Broad Street were originally built for the captains of the packet ships. In this cobbled area, the three young trees were planted by private subscribers to celebrate the coronation of Edward VII and Queen Mary, the subscribers' names were placed on a brass plaque on the protective cage, long since rotted away, although one was saved a few years ago and stored away in the local museum, dating this picture to around 1905.

Above: Approaching The Square from the quays, this is Quay Hill. On the left is the Swan Inn at the top of Bow Hill when Samuel Goodman was landlord around 1900 when this picture was taken. This was the area where many people were killed during the Second World War. Behind the large building on the right, the Church Institute (also destroyed) is The Green where ten people lost their lives. The houses on the left were also destroyed during the same raid.

Left: Norman S. Furneax, a shipping agent and broker whose office was on The Quay, has had an office since after the Second World War. Seen here outside the Anchor Hotel is Betty Bates (with crossed legs), N. Furneax and Mary Peters in 1938.

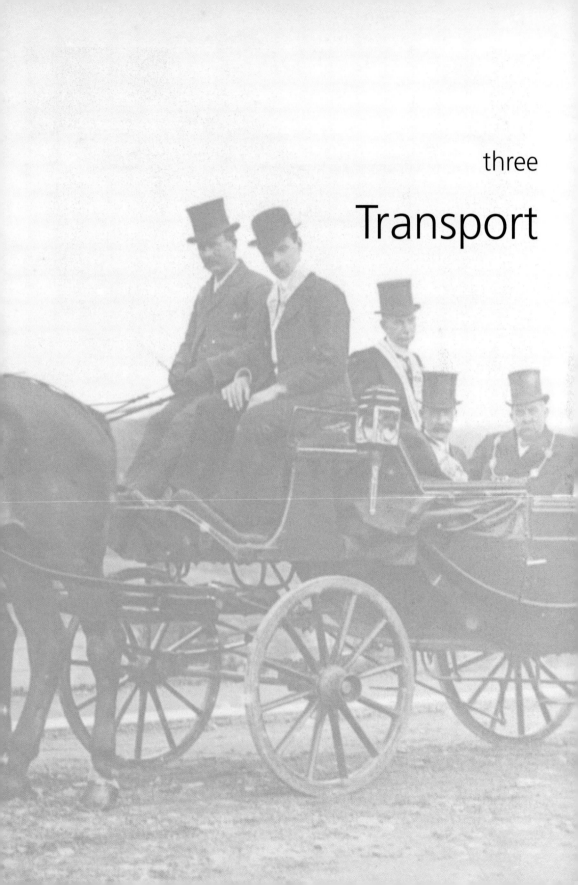

three

Transport

I believe this is an outing for the gentlemen of the Oddfellows of Penryn around 1900, who are dressed in their finest clothing. The driver of this two-horse open Landau is named Lenderyou, the rest include Fred Richards, a young C. W. Andrew (standing), W. J. Martin (sitting), W. A. Platt and Harold Cox. All with either a bowler or top hat. Imagine driving in the dark with candle lamps!

Falmouth Model Laundry taken near to The Square where the Jeals who owned the laundry lived before moving to College House to be near their business. Looking towards Broad Street, this well loaded two-horse wagon could be going to the seaside for a works' day outing. Everyone wears a hat and they sit on bench-type seats known as toast-rack seating. They no doubt came home late having had a lovely day.

Standing proudly alongside their horse and wagon from right to left: 'Mac' Stanley Jeal, son of the owner and manager William Jeal, 'Chappy Benny' and 'Ebbie' Collins. Although named Falmouth Model Laundry the works were at Penryn College Hills. As it reads on top of the wagon, Winners of All England Championship, they won all types of silver cups and medals year after year for their excellent work competing with larger laundries from all over England.

Helston to Falmouth horse-drawn bus stopped outside the Gentleman's Club next to the Penryn Supply Stores of Martin & Son. To the right is the King's Arms. From this bus in 1906 came Dickie Paul and his family from Porthleven, to open Penryn's first fish and chip shop at No. 107 The Terrace selling all types of fish at 1d a piece. See my first book on Penryn for the full story.

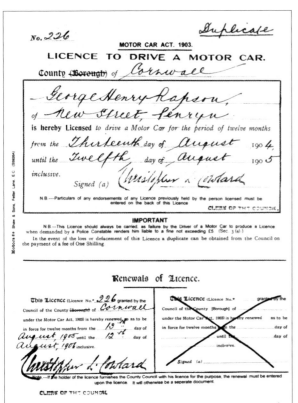

No. 226   Duplicate

MOTOR CAR ACT. 1903.

LICENCE TO DRIVE A MOTOR CAR.

County (Borough) of *Cornwall*

George Henry Rapson,
of *New Street, Penryn*

is hereby **Licensed** to drive a Motor Car for the period of twelve months
from the *Thirteenth* day of *August* 190*4*
until the *Twelfth* day of *August* 190*5*
inclusive.
Signed (a) *Christopher L. Cowlard*

N.B.—Particulars of any endorsements of any Licence previously held by the person licensed must be
entered on the back of this Licence
CLERK OF THE COUNCIL.

IMPORTANT

N.B.—This Licence should always be carried, as failure by the Driver of a Motor Car to produce a Licence
when demanded by a Police Constable renders him liable to a fine not exceeding £5 (Sec. 3 (4).)
In the event of the loss or defacement of this Licence a duplicate can be obtained from the Council on
the payment of a fee of One Shilling.

Renewals of Licence.

This Licence (Licence No.* *226* granted by the
Council of the County (Borough of *Cornwall*
under the Motor Car Act, 1903) is hereby renewed to as to be
in force for twelve months from the *13th* day of
August, 1905 until the *12th* day of
August, 1906 inclusive.

Christopher L. Cowlard

Note.—If the holder of the licence furnishes the County Council with his licence for the purpose, the renewal must be entered
upon the licence. It will otherwise be a separate document.

CLERK OF THE COUNCIL

Left: Licence to drive a motorcar issued to George Henry Rapson of Penryn, a real pioneer of motoring as it was only the 266th licence to be issued in Cornwall. It had to be renewed every year.

Below: At the Norway Inn, here is George Rapson driving a 1904 De Dion Bouton belonging to Dr Beane (Standing next to the policeman with his wife and two children). The other passenger in the car is a motor dealer Mr Eddy. Mr Dawe, a fruit and vegetable merchant, sits in the side car of the motorcycle believed to be an Opal. The car AF 156 runs on pneumatic balloon tyres, brakes only on the rear wheels, no hood or windscreen for weather protection and a lovely pair of brass Lucas King of the Road oil lamps; it also has a boa constrictor horn. The car is meant to carry four people and it only has a single cylinder engine of 8hp. I know, I own an 1903 version.

NORWAY HOTEL.

AF. 156

The inside of Mr Eason's garage. It is hard to date but it shows an early Rudge Whitworth motorcycle behind a wooden car wheel so it could be from around 1910/12 or earlier.

A Darracq motorcar taking part in a Penryn carnival winning first prize and once owned by Mr Eason in July 1912. It was being driven by Miss Chegwidden with her father alongside ten years later in July 1922.

The same car as before, AF 866. Like the De Dion Bouton, it was built in France although the company was financed in England during the golden period (1905-35). It has a 15hp four-cylinder engine costing £275 and new carbine lights and a hood for weather protection.

This Studebaker 20/25hp, AF 1139 once owned by Col. Faulkner-Brown of Tremough, Penryn. It is seen here at Truro Station during the First World War transferring the wounded to the Royal Infirmary after they came off the train. This American car built in 1913 has a gas headlamp missing and a little dent in the rear mudguard.

AF 571 18hp Lacre used by the Falmouth Steam Laundry who had works at The Praze. It had all the water that was needed, which flowed from a stream from Treluswell. The company also did dry cleaning and steam carpet-beating. The works' telephone number was No. 7 with the head office at Church Street, Falmouth. The manager when this vehicle was in use was Pearce Rodgers. The driver with the long coat is named Bert Matthews and the other man is Ted Wills. The vehicle was first bought by the owner Mr Rickard in July 1910 and was chain driven to solid tyres on the rear wheels.

Believed to be owned by William Jeal, owner of the Falmouth Model Laundry, this bus AF 6300 ran between Penryn and Falmouth, regularly seen here in 1926. Ten years earlier when it was bought new, it had electric lights and would only hold up to approximately eighteen people – the luggage went on the roof.

Traffic jam in the main street of Penryn in the mid–1920s. The unused postcard shows RL 1096, a bus owned by the Penryn & Falmouth Motor Co. To the left AF 9360 is a delivery van owned by Mr Dunstan whose ironmongery shop can be seen on the right with the sun blind extended. In the background between the trees and the lamp post is another bus CO 9766. Waiting for passengers, it is an American Rio registered in Plymouth in around 1920 and owned by Willie George of the Pelere Motor Co. Both buses were used on the Penryn to Falmouth route.

The Falmouth Road with the swing bridge to the left of the trailer around 1905. The traction engine pulling stone could quite easily have been the same engine that came to grief at Hill Head after a brake failure a few years later. It belonged to John Freeman, seen here outside the stone works alongside the Penryn River.

Freeman's had quite a number of their own steam traction engines, believed to be made by Foden. This engine is being loaded with huge granite stone which will be taken to Freeman's Yard in Penryn.

Probably the same engine involved in the accident at Hill Head mentioned earlier. It finished its days discarded in a Mabe stone quarry owned by Freeman's.

A Marshall steam road roller 6hp 'S' type registered in Cornwall in 1937, DAF 560, weighing 12 tons. Bought new by R. Dingle & Son of Stoke Crimsland, the company owned it until 1961 when it was sold to G. Connolly & Co. at Falmouth Docks. In 1968 J.H. Pengelly of Penryn bought and restored it from a distressed state to the wonderful condition 'Hilda' is in today. Seen here in Camborne, R. Richards owned the engine for a short time then sold it to Mr C. Thomas of Falmouth who now proudly owns this pride and joy. He uses it regularly and takes it to local shows.

A 1934/35 Austin 7 Ruby registered in Cornwall and used by the Penryn Salvation Army officers. Sitting in the driver's seat is a friend of Captain Samson. The car was made in Longbridge and sports 19-in wheels. The first type of Austin 7s were made for the working class in 1922, seating four people and costing less than £100. Thousands were made and hundreds still exist. I once owned a 1925 soft top and a 1930 saloon more than twenty years ago.

Mrs Brimicombe sitting in an early 1930s Coventry-made Triumph Super Seven with wire wheels and electric lights. The Brimicombes owned a grocer shop which also sold wine and spirits on Fish Cross at the top of New Street for a number of years.

Four Cross Garage, Treluswell, around 1950 and owned by Fred Ball and his two sons, John and Geoff. They carried out repairs and sold Regent petroleum of all grades – 4s 1d for Commercial, 4s 6d for Super and 4s 7d for Supreme. They also sold Redex and Havoline oil to keep the engine running smoothly. In those days all the items garages sold were mainly for motoring. As soon as the car stopped an attendant came out to fill up the car with fuel and dipped the engine for the oil level. There was free air if the tyre pressures were low. The globes on the top of the petrol pumps were made of glass and lit up when dark. On the right is an Austin Princess.

How many local people can remember the traffic lights at Treluswell? Sunnyside B & B is still there, the lights are behind the sign board. Across the road that leads to Truro is a motorcycle and sidecar outside the Automobile Association box and even the 'keep left' signs are different to those of today. The road to the left goes to Redruth. Four Cross Garage is 50 yards to the right leading to Penryn. I was at sea as an engineering officer and was a smoker. One day, whilst in New Zealand, I ran out of cigarettes ashore and went to a kiosk to buy some. Waiting to be served, I heard two men talking about traffic lights just up from the garage and one of them said he had read it in the *Packet*. He mentioned the brewery and then I clicked – the men could not believe it when I said I came from Penryn – one man had lived near the garage and had emigrated and the other came from St Ives.

A 1934 Vauxhall De Luxe light six 15hp seen here with Tony Kerslake, my cousin, who lived at Pencoose Farm. The car was made in Luton and cost £195 when new. The spare wire wheel was located in the front wing giving room for a luggage rack to the rear. Unfortunately this model has a wheel hub missing. The car was used to transport milk churns from the farm to the end of the lane to await collection by the milk lorry.

A Morris Minor convertible outside the workshop and garages of J.C. Annear in Commercial Road, Penryn. It is being driven by 'Doc' Kitts who, with Percy Brokenshire, Bill Tremayne and apprentice Peter Tremougth, were employed as mechanics in 1960 when the photograph was taken. The first of these cars came out in 1952 with an amalgamation of Austin and Morris forming the British Motor Corporation.

Thelma Arnold seen here was a conductress with the Pelere Motor Buses in the 1950s when this photograph was taken.

The type of bus on which Thelma issued her bell-punched tickets – a Leyland acquired in 1949 by Pelere Motors. This is an ex-Devon & General owned by Harold George and is seen here on The Moor at Falmouth. George was an apprentice with Collins & Williams at Ponsharden as a motor mechanic when his father started the Pelere motor business in the 1920s. Harold was put in charge of the buses that ran regularly between Penryn and Falmouth.

A Bedford utility bus HAF 165 owned by Pelere Motors, outside the Town Hall on The Moor at Falmouth. Freddie, Harold's brother also had a bus and worked the same route every ten to fifteen minutes. The company's repair garage was in Commercial Road, Penryn. One of the drivers, Dickie Kneebone would only let people stand on the bus after passing the policeman at the entrance to the Prince of Wales Pier. The last bus from Falmouth departed when the *National Anthem* was played and everyone left the cinema (I walked the two miles to Penryn many a time).

With the opening of the new branch line on 21 August 1863, 700 passengers travelled in thirteen carriages from Truro to Falmouth. Before arriving at Penryn Station, the train passed over the Pascoe Viaduct, the penultimate wooden bridge to be built in the 1860s and locally known as the Tremough Viaduct. The granite pillars on which the wooden fan-type bridge was built still remain at the rear of Harbour View. The viaduct was demolished and replaced with an embankment during the alterations to the Penryn Station in the 1920s.

The last wooden viaduct to be built was known as the College Woods Viaduct and was designed by Isambard Kingdom Brunel. Looking at the bridge to the left it appears that there is a new pile of wood and it that some of the bridge's wood has been replaced. This would date the photograph, taken from an early glass slide, to around 1880. The panoramic view is magnificent, overlooking Penryn and down the river to Flushing on the far left. A rather large three-masted ship is tied up at the quay and the chimney stacks of meads, the Bone & Manure factory and Fox Stanton are prominent.

On the evening of the opening of the branch line, a banquet was held to which 300 guests were invited including all the principal gentry of Cornwall. No one, not even the mayor, was invited from Penryn.

Under the wooden viaduct are piles of stones in preparation for the building of a more permanent bridge. This picture shows a goods train pulling thirteen carriages.

The viaduct was 946ft long and stood 102ft above College Woods. It was constantly being repaired and so was replaced by one made of concrete and granite. An elderly lady once told me she would close her eyes every time she went across the rickety bridge. Not only was it made of wood and wire, it was also built on a curve as can be seen on the postcard.

Starting to build the new structure alongside the wooden viaduct, 6 June 1933. Shaped granite blocks were used for the outside of the piers into which steel rods were inserted and the whole filled with concrete for reinforcement.

Half-built stone piers around 50ft high, October 1936. Looking at the old wooden bridge it is a tangle of wood and wire – it won't be long in place before it is removed.

April 1934 and a number of arches have been built. Scaffolding is still in place as is the wooden viaduct still in use on the other side.

From the top of the arches a group of stone masons are working. The old wooden bridge can be seen on the left, which is still being used whilst the new stone bridge is being built.

Above: June 1934, the viaduct is nearly completed and most of the scaffolding has been removed. The lines were laid on the new bridge.

Below: Demolition of the waiting room on the up line. When the station was first constructed in the mid-1880s it was built in the form of an 'S' without a straight line. In the 1920s it was decided to remove the curved track, replacing it with straight lines. A major reconstruction scheme was implemented which involved removing hundreds of tons of soil. The earth and soil was used to replace the Pascoe Viaduct with an embankment. Trains still ran to Falmouth whilst this work took place, unlike today when a bus would run a shuttle service for the smallest reason.

Arthur Pomery, station master and Ivor Dodd, junior porter at Penryn Station in 1945. The (private) gates at each end of Station Road were opened at 6 a.m. for the first freight train by Vic Williams, a signalman from Truro, and were closed and locked each day at 11 p.m. The three happy GWR workers from left to right: Russell Harvey, Emlin Tidball and Doug Rose.

Carrying 400 people, the first passenger train came through to Penryn filled with mainly Falmouth dock workers ready to start work at 7.30 a.m. At one time Penryn Station employed twenty-five to thirty men. Taken in 1948, GWR workers from left to right: Cecil Tregidgo, Russell Harvey, Douglas Rose, Albert Symons, Howard Jolly.

Penryn Station from the top end of Station Road. It is one of the few buildings left standing after the reconstruction of the whole station during the 1920s. Built by Oliver & Sons of Falmouth it is similar in shape and design to other station buildings in Cornwall. The huge chimneys were for coal fires in the offices and waiting rooms, when Mr Pomery was station master in the late 1940s.

Outside the dry store in the marshalling yard at Penryn in the 1950s. It shows the standard design throughout the GWR for loading and loading carriages; they would be pushed inside and worked on. The store ran alongside the road (to the right in the picture) to take advantage of loaded lorries having to wait. Inside there were small cranes and a weighing machine.

Above: Engine No. 5538 at Penryn Station around 1955. The steam engine and carriages are on the down line to Falmouth. Two people are waiting for the up train on the other side of the platform.

Left: Approaching Penryn Station, this steam engine No. 5562 and two carriages makes its way to Truro moving to the up line from the single track from Falmouth, having just passed over the College Viaduct. The line on the left is part of the elevated goods yard headshunt.

four

Schools, Granite

Penryn Church of England School, *c.* 1910. There was a grammar school attached to Glasney College in medieval times which continued after Henry VIIIs Reformation. Its purpose would have been to teach largely Greek and Latin. The schoolmaster was paid £6 18s a year. Another grammar school is recorded at the same time; the master was John Arscot who was paid £10 annually. Queen Elisabeth I commissioned a grammar school, thought to have been sited near the Bowling Green. References to the grammar school appear in documents dated 1666 and 1715. It closed in 1801. A Methodist school opened in Chapel Lane in 1813 and became the Penryn Primary School. Affiliated to the Church of England, a school was built in 1837 in Commercial Road and was known as the National School. 1848 saw another school built alongside the Methodist school; eventually the two combined and became known as the Council School.

Back row, from left to right: Miss L. Adams, Miss Jenner, Miss A, Hoskin, Miss Mason, Miss Spargo, Mr T. Gill, Miss Frost. Front row: Miss Weir, Mr W.E. Kneebone, Miss Mitchell.

There were several private schools in Penryn especially in the Broad Street area. This photograph was taken around 1910 of Miss Hill's school. It must have been examination or carnival time as no one is smiling, not even William Brimacombe to the right of Miss Hill.

Penryn Council School, *c.* 1952. Back row, from left to right: V. Keast, A. Payne, D. Nicholls, Miss K. Gribble, J. Share, R. Goodman, S. Prout. Middle row: R. Evans, E. Davis, L. Jago, N. Winnon, E. Curtis, S. Quintrill. Front row: R. Crane, D. Annear, C. Welch, S. Mooney.

Penryn Infants School, *c.* 1949. Back row, from left to right: -?-, R. Penhalurick, B. Dunstan, H. Collins, G. Barnicoat, C. Johns, A. Treglown, B. Stevens. Second row: M. Champion, -?-, C. Gilbert, J. Jackson, P. McCartney, C. Kneebone, J. Trengove, R. Stone, A. Cudd, M. Watson, J. Whitford, G. Penhalurick. Third row: E. Davis, A. Cornish, M. Richards, C. Eva, J. Harry, M. Cockrill, M. Stanton, E. Boase, -?-, S. Toy, -?-, T. George, J. Toy. Front row: P. Gedye, D. Sims, B. Sanders, C. Welch, J. Miller, R. Hoskin, T. Jago.

Above: Penryn Church of England School (girls) 1921. Back row, from left to right: I. Williams, -?-, M. Young, M. Thomas, -?-, R. Martin, A. Jago. Second row: V. Warne, -?-, G. Bolitho, B. Tregidgo, L. Travers, V. Hennah, M. Treleaven, L. Ferris, M. Opie, G. Bartlet, Miss Weir. First row: I. Williams, P. Ball, R. Bolitho, I. Coombe, G. Phillips, R. Ferris, M. Jago, D. Timmins, I. Smith. Front row: P. Bartlett, K. Warne, A. Coombs, C. Phillips, N. Ferris, P. Tregidgo, L. Jago, S. Coombs.

Above: Church of England School, class VII for boys, *c.* 1913. Although the boys are dressed alike and wearing hobbed-nail boots, there is one youngster that stands out above the rest. The young man holding the board is named George Collins. On the way to school one morning he had an accident with a horse and cart and was taken to hospital. His leg was so badly injured it had to be amputated. However, it didn't stop him learning and when he left school he sought an apprenticeship with a boot and shoe repairer. George eventually had his own shop in St Thomas's Street selling ice cream during the summer and fruit and vegetables in the winter.

The school teacher is Mr Tommy Gill.

Opposite below: This private school of Miss O'Brien in Broad Street with only eight pupils. Six young ladies are wearing their school hats; the two who are hatless are brother and sister, Norma and John (believed) Evans. Taken in the back yard of Trefalgar House, *c.* 1930s.

Church of England School, 1936–1937. The Praze Academy! Top row, from left to right: R. Binney,
R. Hosking, S. Williams, B. Behenna, E. Rundle, B. Greenwood, A. Bray, B. Churcher, G. Buckingham.
Middle row: R. Bickford, O. Palmer, M. Robins, M. Shepperd, Q. Hutson, B. McCall, G. Gilbert,
E. Pascoe, P. Rundle, P. Gainey. Front row: T. Bickford, L. Webber, W. Hosking, D. Binney, D. Carter,
R. Binney, P. Richards, S. Webber.

Mr Nicholls was Master when this photograph was taken of the Church of England School in the mid-
1950s Standing, from left to right: B. Churcher, A. Wills, J. Killiams, J. Tregonning, P. Williams, G. Rickard,
D. Vincent, J. Sloggett. Sitting: M. Treglown, P. Matterson, H. Barnicoat, B. Kerslake.

Church of England School Football Team, 1951/52. Standing: Mr Nicholls (headmaster), B. Richards, B. Churcher, J. Williams, G. Bate, G. Sloggett. Sitting: M. Smith, W. Burnett, P. Smith (captain), D. Williamson, L. Tregonning.

School prefects, Penryn Secondary Modern School, Quarry Hill, Falmouth, 1957. Back row: D. Rickard, C. Jones, P. Grey, –?–, M. Williams, H. Hodges, M. Bird. Middle row: D. Wills, M. Boase, J. Pellow, C. Kivell, S. Keen, S. Hutchings. Front row: R. Arthur, –?–, M. Maloney, A. Wells, M. Morris, D. Smith.

School prefects, Penryn Secondary Modern School, Quarry Hill, Falmouth, 1958. Back row, from left to right: M. Bird. P. Grey, G. Osborne, -?-, H. Hodges, M. Boase, A. Spargo. M. Williams, J. Bennetts, S. Hutchings. Front row: J. Pellow, R. Arthur, M. Retallack, C. Jones, C. Wright, M. Morris, M. Foreward, -?-. A. Wells, D. Smith.

Penryn Wesleyan Infants School Group III, *c.* 1905. Seven pupils are staning on a form at the back, six boys and one girl. Eight scholars are standing in the second row; the third boy in the row is named George Pellow and the boy on the end is pretending to be a soldier. Seven youngsters are seated, one little girl proudly holding the slate board next to the only little boy in the row. The headmaster was Isaac Manger; the young lady teacher could be Miss Tucker, but what about the lovely hat she's wearing?

JOHN FREEMAN & SONS,
GRANITE QUARRIES,
PENRYN, PENZANCE, & CHEESEWRING,
CORNWALL.

GRANITE of any dimensions, and of Qualities suitable for all Engineering, Architectural and Monumental Purposes, either SCAPPLED, DRESSED, or POLISHED.

SPECIMENS & PRICES FORWARDED ON APPLICATION AT THE OFFICES,

PENRYN, CORNWALL,

9, UNION COURT, OLD BROAD STREET, LONDON;

AND AT

Messrs. W. & J. R. FREEMAN, 27, Millbank St. Westminster

PORTLAND STONE, SERPENTINE, MARBLE, &c., ALWAYS IN STOCK.

When John Freeman came to Penryn in the 1800s, he bought land alongside the river. This photograph was taken from a glass slide and shows the early days at the works. Two horses are pulling a heavy cartload of granite stone through the mud. The open working sheds are in place as is the overhead gantry. There wasn't a crane on the gantry when this slide was taken around 1890.

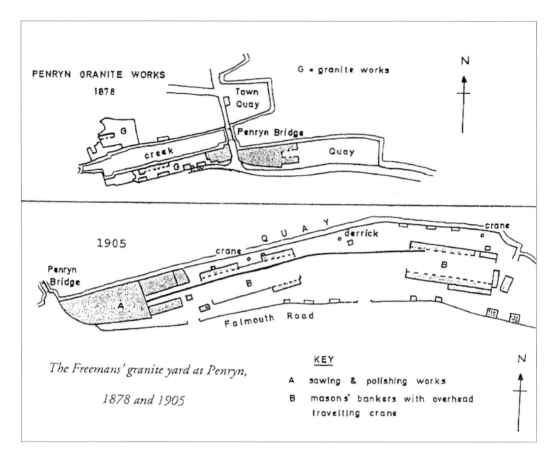

PENRYN GRANITE WORKS
1878

G = granite works

N

Town
Quay

Penryn Bridge

creek

Quay

1905

Penryn
Bridge

Q U A Y

crane

derrick

crane

B

B

A

Falmouth Road

The Freemans' granite yard at Penryn,

1878 and 1905

KEY

A   sawing & polishing works

B   masons' bankers with overhead
    travelling crane

N

Above: Outline drawings of the granite works – the top one is dated 1878 and the bottom one 1905. They show where in Penryn the works were situated alongside the river, where the sawing and polishing sheds are and where the mason's bankers are working with the help of an overhead crane.

Left: A rare photograph of the Cheesewring Quarry taken in 1929 belonging to Freeman's. Stone from the quarry was used to build Westminster Bridge in London, parts of the Royal Naval Dockyard in Plymouth and many other projects throughout the British Isles. Left to right: Bert Mildren, Dick Hooper, Dick Frances, John Hocking–Basset, Tom Hooper.

This colossal granite block weighted 2,738 tons and was blasted out with 119lbs black powder at Polkanuggo Quarry at Mabe in September 1902. No other granite quarries in the United Kingdom can provide blocks of such large dimensions and such uniform grade and faultlessness as are obtained from the Cornish Quarries.

The same stone and quarry taken from further away. A crane to the left would not be large enough to lift this huge piece of granite and it must have been broken into smaller pieces to be managed easier.

Some of the quarrymen at Tinpit Quarry, Mabe. It is thought that Tom Spargo is the third from the left. I would have thought the gentleman on the extreme right was the 'ganger' or foreman, or perhaps it is the man with the bowler hat and long coat on the extreme right.

Using compressed air for polishing these huge granite stones in the 1920s. The men operating the machines wore some protective clothing when they were working. This was a highly skilled job with many workmen coming from the Penryn district. Hundreds of men were employed at Freeman's Yard and in the quarries in the outlying villages.

A diamond-tipped saw cutting a large granite block before it goes into another part of the works to be shaped and completed. Bill Thomas seen here is wearing his 'sack towser' apron at Freeman's Granite Works Yard in Penryn, *c.* 1930.

A belt-driven lathe with a large length of granite being roughly turned into a column before being removed and sent to another part of the works to be dressed and finished. Freeman's had a belt-driven stone lathe as early as 1868 which was still being used as late as the 1940s. This large lathe could take granite up to 24ft long and 4ft in diameter, with gaps for turning basis up to 6ft 6in diameter.

Left: This column has been finished after being turned on the lathe and fluted, the first part at the top has been made separately by an experienced stone mason, dry assembled and then inspected by the yard foreman. Fine examples of these columns can be seen at Godolphin house near Helston.

Below: With the belt-driven lathes on the right of this picture lying idle, it shows the fine examples of the work produced in the workshops. The overhead travelling lifting beam still has a chain around one of the columns. There appears to be a chalk board at the end of this enclosed shed, perhaps to remind the workman of the sizes of columns they are working on.

Freeman's Higher Yard, Penryn, showing stacks of hollow quoins ready to be shipped to various docks throughout England, c.1930. The overhead gantry with the steam crane is seen with two three-masted ships waiting to be loaded.

Freeman's Yard showing stonemasons at work using pneumatic air tools. An American invention, they were first demonstrated in 1895 and were an immediate success. They were also manufactured in Britain previously, however with all the work being carried out by hand it was extremely hard work.

Albert Webber skilfully dressing a large granite block as part of a job for Walton Waterworks using a pneumatic chisel in the mid-1950s. Work with these air tools was always carried out in open sheds because of the dust they threw up, some of which can be seen on Albert's trilby.

These huge blocks of solid granite are being formed into lions' heads. They are resting on large quoins at Freeman's Yard and have been shaped by George Penhalarick on the left and Ernie Webber on the right. They were made for the Royal London House where they can still be seen today.

The lions' heads in position at Finsbury Square. They were made for the London Friendly Society's new premises and the architect was John Belcher. Freeman's must have supplied more than the lions' heads for this job.

Widening of Putney Bridge, London, March 1936. Inside the bridge are Freeman's huge blocks of solid granite and bulks of timber for the alterations. In the centre background the three men are working with a gigantic piece of stone.

Albert Webber holding a small chisel and watching Tom Moore use a pneumatic drill in the 1930s whilst using Freeman's granite for widening Putney Bridge.

Albert Webber with an example of his wonderful crucifix made from granite from Freeman's Yard, Penryn, for a Liverpool Cathedral in the mid-1950s. The company were so proud (and quite rightfully so!) of this work of art that they used it for advertising in their brochures.

The inverted dome for the Queen Elizabeth memorial, Calcutta India, dry set in Freeman's Yard, Penryn. Each stone is lettered, numbered and inspected before being shipped to India.

Dry set in Freeman's Yard is the base of the lighthouse for Tyne North Pier, *c.* 1906.

Freeman's also made the Fastnet Lighthouse. Seen here is the balcony course, dry set for inspection. The granite came from the Cheesewing, Bodmin. The total number of stones in the tower of the new Fastnet Lighthouse is 2,074, having a net cubic content of 58,093 cu. ft and a weight of 4,300 tons. The gross measurement on which the contractor was paid amounted to 72,624 cu. ft. The weights of the individual stones vary from 1¾-3 tons. In addition to this 4,500 cu. ft of small squared blocks were used to fill in holes in the foundation and the spaces between the rock and the tower, up to the level of the entrance gallery. The entire tower was erected in sections of six to eight courses at a time at the contractor's yard in Penryn, and inspected there by either Mr Douglass, or Mr Foot, the resident engineer, before shipment. The top course of each setting was retained to form the bottom course of the next setting, and the gunmetal shutter frames were all fitted in their places when the courses were erected in the contractor's yard, so as to reduce the amount of stone cutting to be done on the rock to a minimum. The stones were set in the yard on strips of sheet lead in the position they would occupy when set permanently on cement beds. It was not necessary to reject any of the stones delivered.

There were twenty pairs of horses used to haul this huge piece of granite from Freeman's Quarry to be transported to Strathfieldsaye. It was to be used for the base of the Wellington monument. It was 9ft x 7ft x 7ft and weighed several hundred tons. The vehicle itself had eight large wheels and the granite was chained around huge blocks of hardwood. There was a large crowd of people lining the route from what is thought to be Mabe Quarry to Penryn when this photograph was taken in 1864.

five

Sports

Penryn owes the forming of a rugby club to J. Marshall Thomas, a watchmaker, regarded as one
of the oldest in Cornwall and formed in 1872. Whilst in London, Thomas played for Blackheath;
back at Penryn he was surprised to see young men in the town quay kicking around a rag ball in
a vaguely rugby fashion. They included stonemasons from Freeman's, barge men, quay workers and
dockers. John Thomas suggested a pig's bladder would serve as a better ball with a canvas covering
to make it last longer. The stem of a clay pipe was used to inflate the bladder. So rugby on an
organised basis was born in Penryn. No one really knows but it is thought that the first match was
between Freeman's Granite Yard and Sarah's Foundry in a field near the Cross Keys public house.

During the 1880s not a club in Cornwall could afford to take Penryn lightly. Between 1885 and
1888 they were the best side around. In 1886 Redruth came to Penryn and played at Green Lane;
Redruth scored a try from the kick-off. When it was disputed, fists began to fly and a free-for-
all ensued, including both sets of supporters. Police were called and arrests were made. Play was
restarted and Penryn scored again and again. Redruth supporters were chased and stoned out of
Penryn. I wonder what happened on the return match at Redruth?

Back row: Charles Wesley Andrew with the trilby hat, Mayor of Penryn. Middle row, fourth
from left: A. Backe, fifth from left: C. Jago; seventh from left: H. Thomas. Front row: R.G. Martin
on the right.

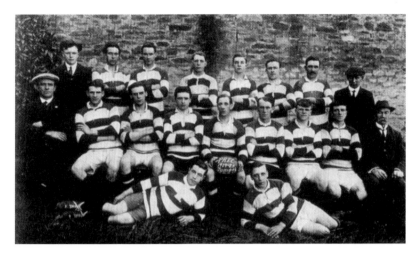

Penryn Reserves, 1919-1920. Back row, third from left: W.J. Shepard, fourth from left: J. Collins, fifth from left: George Jago. Middle row, first from left: George Pellow. Third row, from left: Philip Dancer. Fourth row, from left: Harold Thomas.

There were some outstanding players on the Penryn side and one of the best was Billy Halls who was not only a ferocious tackler but a good kicker of the ball. In the late 1800s he won a competition that was open to the entire United Kingdom. Five pounds was offered by the magazine *Answers* to the player who could kick a rugby ball the farthest. With a heavy leather ball it could soar to a distance of nearly 80 yards, how far would it go with the light plastic ball used to play with today?

The Chiefs, 1923-24. Back row, fifth from left: Dr Hooper; sixth from left: C.W. Andrew. Middle row, third from left: G. Jago, fifth from left: C. Jago; sixth from left: R.J. Martin, seventh from left: W. Sheppard. Front row: E.E. Richards (arms folded); Boy mascot: David Martin.

With a massive slump in Cornish mining and at the town's granite industry, many of the Penryn players emigrated. Those that stayed behind played on with a new name, 'Green Albion', with Billy Pinch as captain. Penryn found their former glory later when Billy Halls returned and they were coached by A.G. Chapman who introduced the three-quarter formation. In the 1911-12 season the club went through a very lean period, nearly packing up when indeed Falmouth club closed down. The jerseys were bought from them for £5 and some Falmouth players came to play at Penryn which made the club carry on until the war.

Roger Hosen playing for Cornwall (as a lad he lived in sight of the Penryn rugby grounds) then he played for Penryn and Northampton, more than fifty times for Cornwall, and ten times for England as a full back. He was a ferocious tackler with a huge kick. During one of the post-war seasons Penryn became the champions of Cornwall and the reserves took the junior title, a joint feat never achieved before. There came a succession of talented young players, George Jago in one season set a club record, scoring 261 points. He was part of Penryn's three-quarters, the best in the county. Another was Eddie Richards; when work took him to Plymouth he played for Plymouth Albion and Devon at least forty times and in 1929 was the first player from Penryn to play for England.

Penryn Rugby Team 1957-58. Top row, from left to right: D. George, P. Oknay; T. Toy, R. Curnow; M. Edwards. First row: B. Bates, B. Young; M. Kneebone, A. Edney; L. Roff, T. Rose. Sitting: M. Keast, P. Head, J. Cobner (captain), P. Williams, A. Ahrans. Front row: B. Mallett, R. Plumber.

After the Second World War the club fielded an attractive side and also, under an enthusiastic band of helpers, set about taking out the gentle slope where they played at Parkengue. B.D. Williams the headmaster of the council school (also the treasurer of the club) had we boys picking up stones with the pretence of giving us free admission for the season. I'm still waiting for it! But it didn't matter, we boys had 'hedge tickets' anyway.

My father, a staunch Penryn supporter especially at home matches, sometimes took my brother and I to see The Borough play at Parkengue. There was one man who we liked to see, the most outstanding player on the field at every match, Victor Roberts. During the Second World War, he worked for HM Customs in Falmouth and rejoined the Penryn Rugby Club. At grammar school he played hooker. Because Penryn's front row was well established, he was selected to play open-side wing forward – that was a really wise move. If you didn't play for either Redruth, Camborne or St Ives, there wasn't much chance for playing for Cornwall. However with the casting vote of the selectors, Victor played for Cornwall. At the next county match at Falmouth he played a blinder in the presence of England's selectors and was selected for the England trials in 1947.

Victor being greeted at Truro Railway Station on his return from his first England match against France in 1947. The greeting party included: Mr and Mrs Jennings, mayor and mayoress, Mrs Roberts, Victor's wife, Nelson Barrett, honorary secretary, George Jago, Jack Chin, Bill Roberts (Victor's brother), Reg Bolitho and members of the Penryn Rugby Football Club.

Between 1947 and 1956 Victor won sixteen England caps. In 1950 he was selected to tour New Zealand with the British Lions. His promotion in the customs service took him away first to Swansea and then to London; he played for both Swansea and Harlequins but never forgot his roots in Penryn.

For the honour that Victor Roberts brought to the town Penryn elected him the Honorary Freeman of the Borough as were Roger Hosen and Ken Plumber, both playing for England, Roger ten times and Ken four. The photograph shows Victor making his speech after receiving the honour, the mayor J.R. Edwards and others including G. Kingdom, J. Chinn, S. Thomas, F. Harris, L. Jenkin, V. Marshall, Mr and Mrs F. Wilde, W. Williams, R. George, K. Blackmore, L. Cambell, Revd J.E. Roberts, B. Jennings, P.T. Dancer, F. Harris and two local reporters.

Also in the picture is the pair of the town's maces and the Jane Killigrew loving cup. To complete the tribute, when my brother was having cancer treatment in Treliske, Victor was there at the same time and took a lot of interest in my brother, being a Penryn man. Even when he was discharged and sent home he phoned several times. On a personal note thank you Victor for the pleasure you gave me when I watched you playing at all levels.

A remarkable boxing club was formed in Penryn in the 1930s. The trainer and promoter was Harold Thomas. Their gymnasium was at the top of New Street and amongst the good boxers were Jack Chinn, Billy Simmons and Eric Blake. Aged just nineteen, the star of the club was Bill Roberts who also played rugby for Penryn like his brother Victor after him. In 1934 he packed the Temperance Hall when he knocked out Bill Jury of St Ives to become heavyweight champion of Cornwall in two rounds. In the same week he was selected for a county rugby trial.

Penryn Netball Team, 1968. Back row, from left to right: B. Drew, M. Richards, J. Drew, H. Scott, D. Rose, S. Symons, H. Ellenbrook. Front row: K. Quintrell, J. Miller, A. Fisher.

Penryn Netball Team is the oldest in Cornwall and originally started as a keep-fit class at the comprehensive school. It was the first appointment of physical education teacher, Jenny Butts. The majority of the class were young mothers who preferred netball to keep fit. In the early days Jenny arranged friendlies with such clubs as Basement, Goonhilly, Penrose and Culdrose. Many of the courts were 'make-do-and-mend' – the one at St Ives actually had to be marked out with chalk. A cast-iron heater encroached on part of Porthleven's court and at Penrose great care had to be taken of the low-slung strip lighting, taking care not to leave the door open on hot evenings in case the ball disappeared down Coinagehall Street! Culdrose was even more of a hazard as we had to negotiate the aerodrome to get to the hangar and more than once one or another has ended up on the runway.

Penryn Netball Club. Back row, left to right: S. Hubber, S. Symons, D. Denivent, G. Hubber. Front row: H. Scott, M. Hilder; K. Quintrell.

By 1974 several teams had been formed throughout the county and it was then that the Netball League came into being. Firstly there was just the one division and at the present time there are six divisions, several clubs sporting more than one team. It was remarked about Penryn's club, 'out of little acorns, big oaks grow!'

The club was very successful, winning the league and most of the numerous tournaments were arranged the county. The club represented the South West, going to Wembley in 1980 and 1981. Through the success we were invited to play many other clubs throughout the South West. One memorable occasion was a tournament at Beaminster and, although we did not win many of our games, we won the award for the 'most sporting team'. The weather was atrocious, some of the teams pulled out but Penryn played on through the torrential rain and thunder and lightning.

Penryn Netball Team. Back row, from left to right: J. Butts, S. Symons, S. Davies, D. Rose, H. Scott, A. Scott, D. Denivent, I. Blackmore. Front row: G. Hubber, S. Hubber, K. Quintrell, M. Kelly, C. Pinhay; M. Hilder.

As with most clubs, funds are always short and there was little in the way of sponsorship in the early days. The team held the odd jumble sale and sponsored walk to get together enough money to buy new kit. The kit was ordered and when it arrived it was minus the 'knickers'. A begging letter arrived from Mencap and the 'knicker money' was unanimously donated so they had to make do and mend. The picture shows a netball team and not a new set of forwards for Penryn rugby team.

Penryn Secondary Modern School's Netball Team in 1958, shortly before the school moved from the Quarry back to the Borough. Back row, from left to right: P. Bettison, Mrs R. Andrew (teacher), J. Jenkins. Front row: C. Kent, R. Evans, V. Keast, E. Boase; S. Quintrell.

Above: The seemingly first-recorded cricket club at Penryn was in May 1878 but it didn't last for long because another more successful one was reformed in April 1881. They played their first match on 4 June at grounds near the railway station against an eleven from Truro where a charge of 1d was made for admission. It was reported that it ended with a victory for Penryn. The scores were Penryn batting first made seventy-three and Truro only thirty-eight. These two small photographs are of Penryn Cricket Club around 1902 when they played at Pencoose. They are not all playing in their 'whites' and even the umpire is wearing a bowler hat. In the top photograph the bowler throws one down. In the bottom picture two batsmen are going for a run.

Right: Penryn versus Mylor, played at Pencoose in May 1922.

CRICKET.

PENRYN V. MYLOR.

Played at Pencoose on Saturday last, May 31st. Scores:—

MYLOR.

L. Lawrence, c. Noye, b. Lovesey	6
W. Rees, b Lovesey	22
W. Nicholls, b. Vawdrey	2
J. Rowe, b. Vawdrey	0
J. Parker, b. Portbury	23
H Moore, b. Hosking	15
E. Lawrence, b. Hosking	2
A. Johns, b. Hosking	5
C. Thomas, b. Portbury	0
J. Frost, not out	0
Curnow, c. Benfield, b. Hosking	2
Extras	22
Total	99

PENRYN.

C. G. Lovesey, c. Moore, b. Lawrence	46
E. S. Griffiths, b. Rowe	0
P. Woolcock, c. L. Lawrence, b. E. Lawrence	1
G. Vawdrey, c. L. Lawrence, b. E. Lawrence	27
R. Hosking. c. Parker, b. E. Lawrence	30
E. J. Portbury, b. Johns	11
A. H. Benfield, not out	10
H. T. Gill, not out	0
Extras	8
Total for 6 wickets	133

E. Noye, E. Travers, F. Chubb did not bat.

PENRYN
Amateur Athletic Sports
WILL TAKE PLACE AT
PARKENGUE, PENRYN,
On SATURDAY (to-morrow), Sept. 10th,

President—C. W. ANDREW, Esq., Mayor.

Vice-Presidents—C. S. Goldman, Esq., M.P., Col. Faulkner Brown, Col. Gray, J.P., Capt. George Read, J.P., J. M. Thomas, Esq., J.P., Dr. Blamey, Dr. Hopper, Charles Stephens, Esq., A. T. Gronwood, Esq., T. Brimacombe, Esq. Starter—Dr. L. B. Hopper. Judges—Capt. G. Read, G. Stephens, Esq., Dr. Rice. Lap Scorers—Messrs. G. W. Andrew, W. Skinner, B. Annear, J. Rapson Timekeeper—Mr. J. M. Thomas.

— SCHEDULE OF EVENTS. —

1. Grand Challenge Walking Match 20 MILES.
For the Championship of Cornwall.
First Prize Value £4 ; Second, £3 10s. ; Third, £2 ; Fourth, £1 10s. ; Fifth, £1 ; Sixth, 10/6. Medals for those covering the course in 3½ hours. Entrance Fee 2/-.

2nd. Mile Flat Race (Open).
First Prize, £1 ; Second, 10/- ; Third, 5/-. Entrance Fee 1/-.

3rd. 100 Yards Flat Race (Open).
First Prize, 10/6 ; Second, 7/6 ; Third, 5/-. Entrance Fee 6d.

4th. One Mile Flat Race. Confined to Members Penryn Football Club.
First Prize, Biscuit Barrel (Presented by C. W. Andrew, Esq.), value £1 ; Second, 10/- ; Third, 5/-. Entrance Fee 6d.

5th. High Jump (Open).
First Prize, 7/6 ; Second, 5/-. Entrance Fee 6d.

6th. ½-Mile Veterans' Race (Handicap).
35 Years or over. 1 Yard start for every Year over 35.
First Prize, 10/- ; Second, 7/6 ; Third, 5/-. Entrance Fee 6d.

7th. Boot and Bottle Race.
Boys under 16. First Prize, 5/- ; Second, 3/6 ; Third, 2/6. Entrance Fee 3d.

8th. Tug of War. Teams to comprise 16 from Falmouth, 10 from Penryn.
Prize 10/- Cash. Entrance Fee 1/- each Team.

9th. Obstacle Race (Open).
First Prize, 15/- ; Second, 10/- ; Third, 5/-. Entrance Fee 1/-.

10th. ½-Mile confined to Forwards P.F. Club.
First Prize, 10/- ; Second, 7/6 ; Third, 5/-. Entrance Fee 6d.

The Walking Match to start from Penryn Town Hall at 1 p.m.

To proceed by way of Quay Hill, Falmouth Old Hill, Harbour Terrace, Quarry Hill, Berkeley Vale, Quarter Mile Lane, Melville Road, Falmouth Station, Bar Terrace, Arwenack Street, Church Street, High Street, Green Bank, Bridge Penryn, Commercial Road, Praze, Brown's Hill, West Street, Town Hall (over same route), as far as Brown's Hill, Treluswell, Four Cross Roads, Treluvre, Mabe, Burnt House, Kernick, to finish with One Mile on the Field.

All Competitors to wear Leather Boots or Shoes with Heels.

Any Competitor cautioned more than twice with more than one Steward will be disqualified. Usual Rules for Walking, Heel and Toe.
No Pacemakers allowed.

Three to compete or no Race. Four to compete where Three Prizes are given.
The decision of the Judges to be final.
All Entrance Fees to accompany Entry, or otherwise not accepted.

☞ ENTRIES CLOSE September 7th, 1910.

ADMISSION 6d. CHILDREN 3d.
A BAND will be in attendance.
First Race on the Field at 3 p.m.

PRIZES to be presented at the Town Hall at 7.30, by
MRS. HOPPER.
F. BELBIN, Hon. Secretary.

Above right: Fred Belbin with the trophies he won as an athlete. He specialised in long-distance walking and was a first-class baker. In *the Commercial, Shipping & General Advertiser* in December 1910 he advertised Christmas cakes, mince pies and confectionary from his premises on The Terrace. In his spare time he kept pigeons and rabbits and at a Bugle show he secured first, third and a special prize for his pointer pigeons and first, special, second and third for his rabbits in August 1919.

Opposite above: Alfred Kerslake owned Pencoose Farm and was always opening bat. With Bernard Bishop more often than not they made two runs, one out and one back. Alf (my uncle) is seen here in action playing for Penryn Cricket Club around 1950. It is not 'Lords' – there is too much grass on the wicket for it to be a test match and the crowds have all gone home. Alf is about to smash a loose one way outside the off-stump for four to six. If he misses, 'Busty Craig' is there to catch it. Longstop has turned his back, he's fed up.

Opposite below: Prize giving for the Penryn Cricket Club around 1950 at the Anchor Hotel. The picture shows Stanley Jewell, Horace Hancock, Bernard Bishop and Alfred Kerslake.

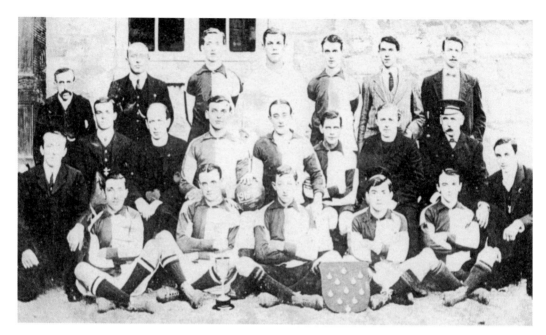

St Gluvias Church Debating Society Association Football Team 1913-1914. Back row, from left to right:
W. Smith, S. Jewell, T. George, S. Williams, S. Carter, R. Hellard, B. Jennings. Middle row: C. Richards,
Revd F.R. Carr (president), F. Richards (hon. secretary), S. Welch (captain), A. Retallick, Revd J.G. Lane-
Davies, W. Pinch. Front row: S. Jewell, J. Mylin, D. Meddling, C. Jago, T.G. Lloyd, C.H. Pearce, C. Pinch.

Penryn Association Football Team around 1920. Back row, from left to right: F. Stanley, -?-, W. Smith,
J. Richards, -?-, T. George, J. Thomas, W. Burleigh, G. Francis, T. Webber. Front row: A. Thomas, L. Hodge,
T. Richards (captain), A. Nother, G. Burleigh.

Glasney Rangers Football Team around 1945. Because of a concrete cover over the sewage system at Glasney field, Glasney Rangers played their home matches in the Penryn and Falmouth District League at a farm in Ponsanooth (under the railway bridge owned by Mr Dunstan). Back row, from left to right: N. Webber, J. Garland, I. Meagor, R. Bolitho, J. Mitchell, I. Scorse, P. Barnicoat, G. Burleigh, J. Scorse, Mr Meagor. Front row: P. Webber, N. Meagor, M. Richards, I. Head, H. Jeffries.

The Commercial Inn Darts Team with their Whitbread Shield and medals they won, c. 1950. Back row, from left to right: J. Jefferies, R. Norris, R. Gardner, F. Chamberlain, C. Young, H. Benny, T. Pearce. Front row: J. Wilkes, M. Jefferies, J. Williams (captain), W. Mitchell, I. Odgers.

Penryn Liberal Club Darts Team, c. 1950. Back row, from left to right: E. Eustace, S. Woodward, L. Jago, T. Jago, E. Riddle. Front row: O. Toy, R. Carey, C. Medley, W. Burleigh.

A cycling club was formed in Penryn as early as April 1881. J. Tregaskis was elected captain and J.H. Trunan secretary and treasurer. This photograph dated to around 1900 shows twenty-seven members of the club plus another lady viewing the scene. The fifteen machines on view all look like safety bicycles which followed 'The Dandy', 'Bone Shaker' and the 'Ordinary' (Penny Farthing). The author owns two of the last three.

Penryn Cycle Club, 1901, with possibly the same members and similar machines and the last image. The bicycles now have paraffin lamps on display. By this date the secretary's name may have changed because a letter dated 1893 from 3, Market Street, Penryn, was signed J.M. Thomas, secretary of The Cyclist Touring Club, Penryn Branch, seen here on an outing.

This Christmas postcard to M.J. Thomas also says Penryn Cycling Club at Enys in sunshine and frost, the same as a couple of words printed on the front of the card. This one could be dated to around 1900.

Above: The Riviera Wheelers, based in Penryn, at Kennack Sands with their bicycles, 1946/47. Standing, from left to right: -?-, E. McCall, E. Bishop, -?-, -?-, F. Brewer, C. Winn. Sitting: G. Burleigh, Alga Burleigh, A. Burleigh.

Left: May 1868 saw the first rowing club formed in Penryn, launching their first boat, a 34ft Skiff built by F. Holmes called 'Challenge'. A forerunner of two or three others, it was a very fast boat. A more recent rowing club was formed by Harry Jennings and Les Hilder, 'The Flying Anchor', being the first boat built by Harry Jennings. It wasn't long before competitive rowing was sought by the club and Robert Hilder entered a crew of youngsters with a boat called 'Celerity', being only 15ft long. The photograph shows Robert Hilder and Michael Gallaway, two oars champions of Cornwall with their trophies around 1960.

Rowing clubs in the rest of Cornwall used 18ft boats so Penryn came up with an ingenious idea of a 3ft extension which enabled them to complete in the Flashback Races. The next regatta Penryn won in the County Gig boat beating top crews from the county and the Plymouth area. Seen here are the members of the rowing club with a boat built by Robert Hilder in the disused Salvation Army Hall. They are: Mark Curnow (cox), Alan Blackmore, Dermot Rees, Dickey Rees.

Later Penryn built their first Flash boat *The Saracen*, again built by Robert Hilder and Michael Gallaway from a design by Percy Dalton. They finished first in the very first tace in a two-oared event. The first four-oared championship was won in a boat called *Bits & Pieces*. For year Penryn continued to win with this boat designed by Tommy Bryant, built again by Robert Hilder, with a fine crew including Colin Blackmore, Alan Blackmore, Dermot Rees and coxed by Mark Curnow. Seen here in this photograph are, from left to right: Harry Jennings, Terry Jennings, John Wright, Granville-Ball (president), David Duckham, Leslie Hilder, Stanley Jewell.

There were other successes for Penryn Rowing Club achieved in the 'Doug Thomas', the 'Sid & Sue' and the 'Angoft', designed and built by club chairman Victor Angrove.

Seen here are Penryn Rowing Club members with trophies from left to right: Philip McCall, Michael Gallaway, David Duckham, Robert Hilder and John Crockford.

Presentation time after another successful Penryn Regatta. The mayor and mayoress, Mr and Mrs J.R. Edwards, flanked on the left by Ernie Medlin and Leslie Hilder (harbour master), are about to present the trophies and prizes won that day at the regatta.

Penryn Rowing Club was a founder member of the Cornwall Rowing Association formed in 1951 and has a uniqueness that two chairmen of the association have been appointed from the club. One was Alan Anderson, the other Les Hilder whose son Robert is a life member of the association. The club is arguably the most successful in Cornwall and has a wealth of experience to draw upon and produce season after season of fine young rowers to continue the tradition.

On or near its original site, the game of bowls has been played in Penryn for hundreds of years. The town's account book (1652-1795) contains several references to the bowling green and the cost of maintaining it. The Public Record Office has an item dated 1546 which refers to a licence being issued to a Rauf Couche to keep bowling and other specified games within Penryn. Over the years it must have petered out because in July 1931, a well-attended meeting in Penryn Town Hall, presided over by J.C. Annear, considered forming a bowling club but had difficulty in finding a suitable site for laying out the green.

The opening of the bowling green in 1954. Back row, from left to right: Mrs Hitchens, Mrs Williams, Mrs Toy, -?-, Mrs Thomas, Mrs Webber. Front row: -?-, Mrs Smith, Miss Truscott, mayor and mayoress, Mr and Mrs J.R. Edwards, Mrs Jennings, Mrs Mancell, Mrs Collings, Mrs Miller; Mrs Treweek.

It was decided to form a club with A.T. Greenwood as chairman and C. Richards, secretary. Nothing more was done until July 1932 when the Chamber of Commerce reported that the Bowling Green Committee had met on the old foundry site which had been suggested as a bowling green but was found to be too small. It was mentioned again at a council meeting in October that Penryn had a lovely park and playground but one thing that was badly needed was a bowling green. There was no more done about this for several years until it came up again in a Penryn Council meeting in August 1935 when Mr P.T. Dancer reported that it was recommended that the council should NOT proceed with the suggested bowling green for Penryn in view of the heavy expenses contemplated in the playing field scheme and other matters.

It is believed the ladies in their white uniforms and hats are members of visiting teams from all over Cornwall on opening day with Mr and Mrs J.R. Edwards.

An advertisement appeared in the *Penryn Advertiser* in August 1935 relating to the forming of a bowling club and once more it was unanimously decided to form a club. A deputation was appointed to wait for the town council with a view of getting that body to provide a green and let it at a yearly rental to the club. J.C. Annear again presided. Representation was made by both Falmouth and Mawnan bowling clubs to give all help and information required. Members of the town council also spoke in favour of the proposal. For the second time J.C. Annear was elected president with H. Rogers as secretary and H. Hunt as treasurer. At the next meeting of the town council it was agreed a deputation should meet the General Purposes Committee.

The photograph shows the first 'wood' to be bowled by Mrs Edwards although somehow I do not feel this is the correct way! Her husband, mayor J.R. Edwards looks on as does Miss Truscott the president. Behind the fencing will be the Memorial Grounds. Jack Mitchell first mowed the grass; when he retired, Michael Churcher took over the task of cutting and keeping the green weed-free until artificial grass was laid in 1972.

A month later at the next council meeting J. Jackson said there seemed to be some feeling in the minds of the rate payers that either The Park or The Green was to be used for the proposed new bowling green. Could they have an assurance that this would NOT happen. The mayor replied that there was no such intention at present and Mr Coad said an endeavour was being made to get some land outside of these places. Once again that was that and I cannot find any other mention of a Bowling Club for Penryn – even that had taken from July 1931 to October 1935. Time went on, the war came, and as we know Penryn was bombed and many people killed. The site was cleared and Penryn had its bowling green. A Memorial Garden was planted and dedicated to those who died behind the bowling club. So it has come full circle –going back to the beginning where it is thought the first game of bowls was played in Penryn.

From left to right: Penryn Ladies, Mrs B. Blacket, Mrs P. Bishop, Mrs F. Miller, Mrs D. Williams. The rest are Falmouth ladies playing at Falmouth.

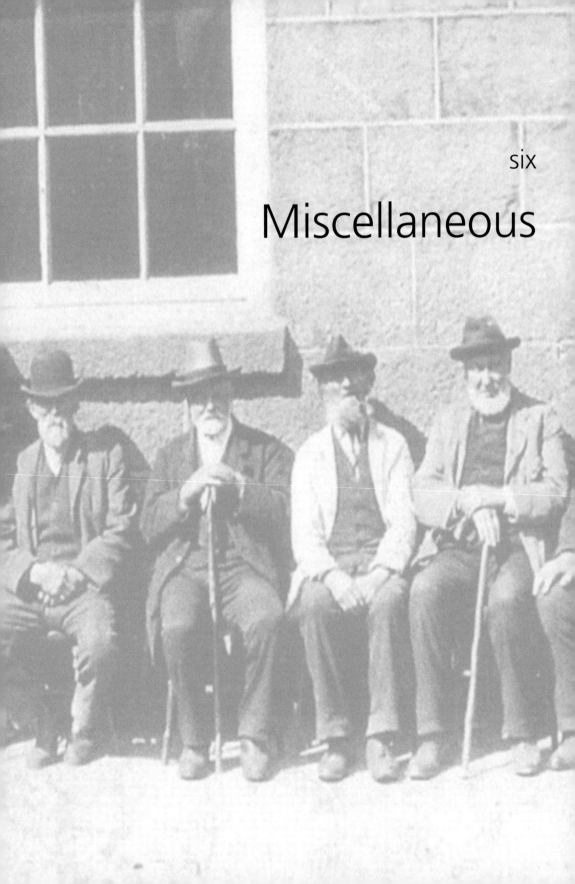

six

Miscellaneous

Penryn Wesleyan Methodist Choir around 1922. Back row, from left to right: E. Davies, W. Edney, C. Mallett, F. Jacket, W. Mallett, T. Pearce, H. Lugg, G. Thomas, F. Chegwidden, F. Roberts, C. Davey. Third row: E. Rapson, M. Pearce, V. Rashleigh, S. Sowden, L. Hall, J. Spargo, A. Spargo, O. Mallett, G. Paul, N. Lovell, M. Chegwidden, K. Fugler. Second row: R. Hutchings, M. Spargo, D. Blight, H. Davies, J. Marshal-Thomas (mayor and choir master), D. Truscott, M. Rapson, D. Pearce, V. Belbin. Front row: H. Davies (organist), C. Lobb, B. Hicks, K. Davey, P.T. Dancer (deputy organist).

Penryn Wesleyan Methodist Sunday school teachers, 1927. Back row, from left to right: F. Lobb, B. Edney, T. Chinn, H. Lugg, B. Hicks, H. Davies. W. Mallett. Third row: N. Furneax, P. Hodge, F. Chegwidden, J. Spargo, F.C. Chegwidden, W. Mallett, A. Spargo, J. Martin, J.C. Mallett, J. Mallett. Second row: P.T. Dancer, B. Opie, J. Lugg, M. Furneax, A. Greenwood, B. Mitchell, M. Rickard. Front row: M. Tresidder, M. Richards, P. Abraham, M. Pearce, H. Edney, E. Hicks, M. Hicks.

The photograph was taken outside Bella Vista House.

When the Royal Cornwall Show came to Penryn in 1873, 11,812 people attended. The president of the show that year was Lord Elliott. The show took place in the fields alongside the house at Roskrow. The photograph shows John Clemens riding 'Lady Penryn' (how appropriate). In 1932 the show came to Carclew where 17,362 people attended.

Penryn Town Council outside the Town Hall in 1946 with the priceless Jane Killigrew Silver Cup. Top row from left to right: W. Pellowe, V. Pascoe, J. Hug, F. Collins, J. James, M. Edmonds, J. Yates. Middle row: B. Richards, J. Harris, S. Thomas, E.L. Jenkins, F. Mountford, J. Simcock, F. Harris, L. Butland, W. Daniel, C. Burleigh. Bottom row: C. Tutton, L. Coad, G. Pellowe, H. Jennings (mayor), T. Greenwood, W. Basher; P.T.Dancer with the priceless Jane Killigrew Silver Cup.

Penryn's mayor and mayoress H.B. Jennings (left front) with mothers and children from Penryn around 1945. Amongst them can be seen Mrs Wright, Mrs Handcock, Mrs Watson, Mrs Riddle, Mrs Foster and Mrs Jenkins.

Some of the workforce of Sara & Burgess's foundry in Commercial Road, Penryn around 1915. I wonder if the gentleman in the suit with his hands in his pockets is either one of the owners or perhaps a foreman. The foundry goes back to at least the 1750s; they made and cast all types of components including complete engines for most of the boats that were built locally. If you read on you will learn they made Hornblower's steam engine that was tested at Enys.

A row of Penryn gentlemen sitting outside the Gentleman's Club and the King's Arms. Every other man has a walking stick, they all wear some type of hat and all have facial hair! This photograph dates back to the 1920s or before.

In the 1930s, because of the increased traffic going over the swing bridge and its continuous repairs, it was decided to move it, widen the roads on both sides and replace the swing bridge with a permanent one. A ship is still being worked upon and an Austin 12/14 is passing over the old swing bridge. The new bridge was opened by Hore-Belisha, Minister of Transport on 14 February 1936. The Mayor of Penryn, Tommy Greenwood, and councillors were present. The contractors were A.E. Farr who worked under the county surveyor, E.H. Collcutt. My mother told me I was the first to cross the bridge, when she wheeled me over in my pram at the age of nine months.

A mail train with passenger carriages was derailed on the evening of Friday 31 August 1898. Travelling at 30-40mph and taking a bend too fast, it left the track, falling down a steep embankment, coming to rest only when the funnel and whistle (see insert) became embedded in the slope. The driver and fireman were taken to hospital and later the driver died of shock. Most of the thirty-three passengers were not injured and a relief train was sent from Truro.

It is written on the roof of the sheds 'Dry Dock Marine Engineers & Ship Repairers'. In the dry dock at Ponsharden (on the Penryn boundary) is an unusual vessel being repaired and its bottom painted. It is a tug owned by the Royal National Lifeboat Institution named Helen Peele from Padstow, being built in Leith in 1901. It has twin screws, measures about 100ft long and has a speed exceeding 10 knots from its twin engines. Seen here after the First World War, three men are watching two men working on the rudder; part of the hull has been painted and the rest awaits a lick of paint. The scaffolding looks a little dangerous to me, I'm sure it wouldn't be allowed today.

Aerial photograph of Penryn, 1924.

Aerial photograph of Penryn, 1960. Compare the difference.

Could this photograph date to Coronation Day in 1953? You know who you are!

Regatta from Quay Hill, with thongs of excited people with flags and bunting, yachts and sailing boats and swing boats on the quay, *c.* 1900. Penryn's first regatta was on July 16 1867, commencing at 1 p.m. for, 'open sailing boats with a first prize of £2 through rowing boats two oars etc, barges belonging to Penryn under 30 tons, rowing skiffs, yawls pulled by sailors from H.M.S. Ganges first prize £5, to gig and punt chase for £1. first prize. No entry fee up to the 13th July 2/- after. A brass band will be in attendance'.

Above left: Penryn had previously supported the Royal Cornwall Regatta held annually at Falmouth, and the town's people were determined to hold one of their own. A committee was formed which included Lavin, Cornfield, Mead, Furneax, Burch, Gill, Cornfield junior as treasurer and Messrs Share and Rowe, secretaries. With great excitement the day came and it rained, however towards noon the skies cleared and by 1 p.m. it was a beautiful day with a fresh breeze. The *Atlanta* belonging to the Union Shipping Co. was used as the committee boat and a pinnace from HMS *Ganges* was used as the winning post. The band of Falmouth Rifle Volunteers attended the event. The scene viewed from the river and banks was picturesque and pleasing, the quays were crowded with people as were the river banks towards Falmouth for a considerable distance. The gig and punt race caused great amusement and the sports concluded with prizes of legs of mutton for the winners of the greasy pole which caused roars of laughter amongst the huge crowds.

This postcard dating to around 1900 shows Penryn Regatta, the ladies dressed in their finest gowns and beautiful fancy hats watching sailing and rowing races.

Above right: At the end of 1879 an advertisement was placed in the *Penryn Advertiser* as follows:

> To Be Disposed of a first class general smithy business with a good stock of iron goods and about ten tons of coal with every requisite for carrying on an excellent trade, possession may be had at once. Also a Superior Cob, five years old price £50. Application to be made to William Dunstan veterinary Shoeing Forge. The Praze. Penryn.

It was bought in January 1880 by James Collett and bought back sometime later by William Dunstan who passed it to Richard Dunstan. On Richard's demise his son Arthur Clarence Dunstan continued the business. The photograph shows 'Dickie' (Arthur Clarence) Dunstan repairing a chisel on his anvil in his workshop at The Praze. He was a lovely, kind man, mayor of Penryn 1973/75 and Master of Three Grand Principles Lodge, Penryn in 1975.

Jonathan Hornblower was born in July 1753 at Chacewater, the fourth son of an engineering family and an engine builder. He was educated at a Truro grammar school before entering an apprenticeship to a plumber or brazier at Penryn, and lived with his parents at Trelever where he was baptised in July 1713. Reading the letter (see next image) it was sent to Davies Gilbert his friend and mentor, it can be seen that he invented and tested a steam engine at Enys in 1796. He had previously erected an engine at Tincroft mine in 1791 which some people said was better than Boulton & Watts, some worse. By 1794 he had erected a further nine engines in Cornwall, in different mines, their designs again near to Watts. He patented two other designs, one in 1798 and the other in 1805 but neither were successful – he was self-opinionated and concentrated too much on his own ideas instead of high-pressure engines where the future lay. In the later years of his life he became disillusioned and became interested in astronomy. His foundry and works at Penryn flourished for he left a large estate just below £10,000 when he died in Penryn on 23 February 1815. What a pity he didn't succeed. If he could have done better than Richard Trevithick (he was years ahead of him), we could be celebrating the Hornblower Day instead of Fair Day.

In 1781, a British patent was taken out for the first compound steam engine by Jonathan Carter Hornblower. His invention was to use two cylinders of equal size attached to the same beam. Steam acts first in a small high-pressure cylinder, leaving at a lower pressure, but still sufficient to expand further in a larger cylinder. Although he claimed greater efficiency, this was not realised at the low steam pressures of the day. Because Hornblower used a separate condenser, it infringed the patent of Boulton & Watts so it was abandoned.

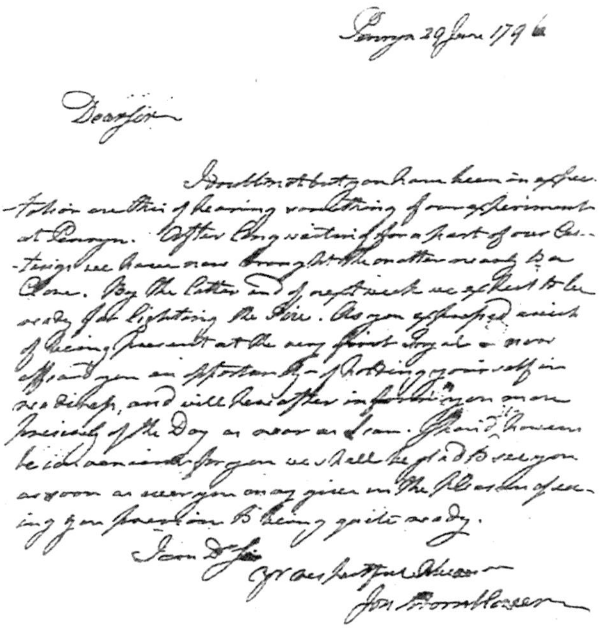

[handwritten letter]

Penryn 29 June 1796

Dear Sir,

Penryn 29 June 1796

Dear Sir,

     I doubt but you have been in expectation ere this of hearing something of our experiments at Penryn. After long waiting for a part of our castings we have now brought the matter nearly to a close. By the later end of the week we expect to be ready for lighting the fire. As you expressed a wish of being present at the very first trial I now afford you an opportunity of holding yourself in readiness, and will hereafter inform you more precisely of the day as near as I can. Should it however be convenient for you we shall be glad to see you as soon as ever you may give us the pleasure of seeing you previous to being quite ready.

    I am Dr Sir
        Your Faithful Servant

        Jon Hornblower.

Other local titles published by Tempus

A Cornish Christmas

TONY DEANE AND TONY SHAW

This fascinating collection of over 200 old images pays tribute to the people who have proudly called Llantrisant their home. Commanding an outstanding setting on the crest of a hill, Llantrisant's splendour lies in its enchanting beauty and celebrated past. Bloodthirsty battles, pioneering acts of cremation and captured kings of England have all played a part in shaping the town, as have the generations of families who have lived here.

978 07524 3974 7

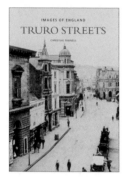

Truro Streets

CHRISTINE PARNELL

Christine Parnell has researched the origin and development of the city's streets from their beginnings through to modern times. As well as an A-Z gazetteer of Truro's streets, the book combines a more formal history of with many amusing tales. Calamitous fishing trips, Louis James Williams who played his barrel organ dressed in a blue and white clown suit and Billy Onions who pumped the bellows for the organ at St Georges Church are sure to delight the reader.

978 07524 4371 3

Haunted Cornwall

PAUL NEWMAN

For anyone who would like to know why Cornwall is called the most haunted place in Britain this collection of stories of apparitions, manifestations and related supernatural incidents from around the Duchy provides the answer. The book features a gory medieval murder at Poundstock; a gruelling exorcism at Botathan; a 'human double' clocking-in for work at St Austell and a phantom stagecoach on the Mevagissey road.

978 07524 3668 5

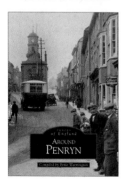

Around Penryn

ERNIE WARMINGTON

The town of Penryn was founded by charter in 1216. Over the centuries which followed, the settlement grew and became an important shipping centre for Cornwall's tin and granite industries, so much so that earned the name of 'the Granite Port'. This intriguing compilation is sure to appeal to all who know Penryn, both young and old. For those who remember how the town used to be, it will be a nostalgic trip into the past.

978 07524 2098 1

If you are interested in purchasing other books published by Tempus, or in case you have difficulty finding any Tempus books in your local bookshop, you can also place orders directly through our website

www.tempus-publishing.com